D0400077

S E R I E S

A NavPress Bible study on the book of

1 THESSALONIANS

BRINGING TRUTH TO LIFE
NavPress Publishing Group
P.O. Box 35001, Colorado Springs, Colorado 80935

OUR GUARANTEE TO YOU

We believe so strongly in the message of our books that we are making this quality guarantee to you. If for any reason you are disappointed with the content of this book, return the title page to us with your name and address and we will refund to you the list price of the book. To help us serve you better, please briefly describe why you were disappointed. Mail your refund request to: NavPress, P.O. Box 35002, Colorado Springs, CO 80935.

The Navigators is an international Christian organization. Our mission is to reach, disciple, and epuip people to know Christ and to make Him known through successive generations. We envision multitudes of diverse people in the United States and every other nation who have a passionate love for Christ, live a lifestyle of sharing Christ's love, and multiply spiritual laborers among those without Christ.

NavPress is the publishing ministry of The Navigators. NavPress publications help believers learn biblical truth and apply what they learn to their lives and ministries. Our mission is to stimulate spiritual formation among our readers.

© 1995 by The Navigators
All rights reserved. No part of this publication may be reproduced in any form without written permission from NavPress, P. O. Box 35001, Colorado Springs, CO 80935.
ISBN 08910-99328

Unless otherwise identified, all Scripture quotations in this publication are taken from the *HOLY BIBLE: NEW INTERNATIONAL VERSION®* (NIV®). Copyright © 1973, 1978, 1984 by International Bible Society. Used by permission of Zondervan Publishing House. All rights reserved.

Printed in the United States of America

3 4 5 6 7 8 9 10 11 12 13 14 15 / 02 01 00

FOR A FREE CATALOG OF
NAVPRESS BOOKS & BIBLE STUDIES,
CALL 1-800-366-7788 (USA)
or 1-416-499-4615 (CANADA)

CONTENTS

ACKNOWLEDGMENTS

The LIFECHANGE series has been produced through the coordinated efforts of a team of Navigator Bible study developers and NavPress editorial staff, along with a nationwide network of fieldtesters.

AUTHOR: RON RHODES
SERIES EDITOR: KAREN LEE-THORP

HOW TO USE THIS STUDY

Objectives

Most guides in the LIFECHANGE series of Bible studies cover one book of the Bible. Although the LIFECHANGE guides vary with the books they explore, they share some common goals:

1. To provide you with a firm foundation of understanding and a thirst to return to the book;
2. To teach you by example how to study a book of the Bible without structured guides;
3. To give you all the historical background, word definitions, and explanatory notes you need, so that your only other reference is the Bible;
4. To help you grasp the message of the book as a whole;
5. To teach you how to let God's Word transform you into Christ's image.

Each lesson in this study is designed to take 60 to 90 minutes to complete on your own. The guide is based on the assumption that you are completing one lesson per week, but if time is limited you can do half a lesson per week or whatever amount allows you to be thorough.

Flexibility

LIFECHANGE guides are flexible, allowing you to adjust the quantity and depth of your study to meet your individual needs. The guide offers many optional questions in addition to the regular numbered questions. The optional questions, which appear in the margins of the study pages, include the following:

Optional Application. Nearly all application questions are optional; we hope you will do as many as you can without overcommitting yourself.

For Thought and Discussion. Beginning Bible students should be able to handle these, but even advanced students need to think about them. These questions frequently deal with ethical issues and other biblical principles. They often offer cross-references to spark thought, but the references do not give obvious answers. They are good for group discussions.

For Further Study. These include: a) cross-references that shed light on a topic

5

the book discusses, and b) questions that delve deeper into the passage. You can omit them to shorten a lesson without missing a major point of the passage.

If you are meeting in a group, decide together which optional questions to prepare for each lesson, and how much of the lesson you will cover at the next meeting. Normally, the group leader should make this decision, but you might let each member choose his or her own application questions.

As you grow in your walk with God, you will find the LIFECHANGE guide growing with you—a helpful reference on a topic, a continuing challenge for application, a source of questions for many levels of growth.

Overview and details

The study begins with an overview of the book of 1 Thessalonians. The key to interpretation is context—what is the whole passage or book *about*?—and the key to context is purpose—what is the author's *aim* for the whole work? In lesson one you will lay the foundation for your study of 1 Thessalonians by asking yourself, "Why did the author (and God) write the book? What did they want to accomplish? What is the book about?"

In lessons two through eleven you will analyze successive passages of 1 Thessalonians in detail.

After you have completed the final lesson, you may want to review 1 Thessalonians, returning to the big picture to see whether your view of it has changed after closer study. Review will also strengthen your grasp of major issues and give you an idea of how you have grown from your study.

Kinds of questions

Bible study on your own—without a structured guide—follows a progression. First you observe: What does the passage *say*? Then you interpret: What does the passage *mean*? Lastly you apply: How does this truth *affect* my life?

Some of the "how" and "why" questions will take some creative thinking, even prayer, to answer. Some are opinion questions without clear-cut right answers; these will lend themselves to discussions and side studies.

Don't let your study become an exercise of knowledge alone. Treat the passage as God's Word, and stay in dialogue with Him as you study. Pray, "Lord, what do You want me to see here?" "Father, why is this true?" "Lord, how does this apply to my life?"

It is important that you write down your answers. The act of writing clarifies your thinking and helps you to remember.

Study aids

A list of reference materials, including a few notes of explanation to help you make good use of them, begins on page 105.

This guide is designed to include enough background to let you interpret with just your Bible and the guide. Still, if you want more information on a subject or want to study a book on your own, try the references listed.

Scripture versions

Unless otherwise indicated, the Bible quotations in this guide are from the New International Version of the Bible. Other versions cited are the New American Standard Bible (NASB) and the King James Version (KJV).

Use any translation you like for study, preferably more than one. A paraphrase such as The Living Bible is not accurate enough for study, but it can be helpful for comparison or devotional reading.

Memorizing and meditating

A psalmist wrote, "I have hidden your word in my heart that I might not sin against you" (Psalm 119:11). If you write down a verse or passage that challenges or encourages you, and reflect on it often for a week or more, you will find it beginning to affect your motives and actions. We forget quickly what we read once; we remember what we ponder.

When you find a significant verse or passage, you might copy it onto a card to keep with you. Set aside five minutes during each day just to think about what the passage might mean in your life. Recite it over to yourself, exploring its meaning. Then, return to your passage as often as you can during your day, for a brief review. You will soon find it coming to mind spontaneously.

For group study

A group of four to ten people allows the richest discussions, but you can adapt this guide for other sized groups. It will suit a wide range of group types, such as home Bible studies, growth groups, youth groups, and businessmen's studies. Both new and experienced Bible students, and new and mature Christians, will benefit from the guide. You can omit or leave for later years any questions you find too easy or too hard.

The guide is intended to lead a group through one lesson per week. However, feel free to split lessons if you want to discuss them more thoroughly. Or, omit some questions in a lesson if preparation or discussion time is limited. You can always return to this guide for personal study later. You will be able to discuss only a few questions at length, so choose some for discussion and others for background. Make time at each discussion for members to ask about anything they didn't understand.

Each lesson in the guide ends with a section called "For the group." These sections give advice on how to focus a discussion, how you might apply the lesson in your group, how you might shorten a lesson, and so on. The group leader should read each "For the group" at least a week ahead so that he or she can tell the group how to prepare for the next lesson.

Each member should prepare for a meeting by writing answers for all of the background and discussion questions to be covered. If the group decides not to take an hour per week for private preparation, then expect to take at least two meetings per lesson to work through the questions. Application will be very difficult, however, without private thought and prayer.

Two reasons for studying in a group are accountability and support. When each member commits in front of the rest to seek growth in an area of life, you can pray with one another, listen jointly for God's guidance, help one another to resist temptation, assure each other that the other's growth matters to you, use the group to practice spiritual principles, and so on. Pray about one another's commitments and needs at most meetings. Spend the first few minutes of each meeting sharing any results from applications prompted by previous lessons. Then discuss new applications toward the end of the meeting. Follow such sharing with prayer for these and other needs.

If you write down each other's applications and prayer requests, you are more likely to remember to pray for them during the week, ask about them at the next meeting, and notice answered prayers. You might want to get a notebook for prayer requests and discussion notes.

Notes taken during discussion will help you to remember, follow up on ideas, stay on the subject, and clarify a total view of an issue. But don't let note-taking keep keep you from participating. Some groups choose one member at each meeting to take notes. Then someone copies the notes and distributes them at the next meeting. Rotating these tasks can help include people. Some groups have someone take notes on a large pad of paper or erasable marker board (preformed shower wallboard works well), so that everyone can see what has been recorded.

Introduction

Paul and Thessalonica

Map of the Roman Empire

The poet Antipater called Thessalonica the "mother of all Macedon."[1] Strabo, the Greek geographer of the Augustan Age, described it as Macedonia's most populous town and the metropolis of the entire province.[2] Indeed, with a population of over 200,000, Thessalonica was widely considered a city to be reckoned with . . . economically, politically, and militarily.

When the Apostle Paul traveled throughout Macedonia on his second missionary tour, he encountered a land of high mountains, broad rivers, and fertile valleys. This area of the world boasted rich farm land and timber, and was well known for its extensive deposits of silver and gold.

Thessalonica had flourished for hundreds of years, largely because of its ideal location on the banks of the Thermaic Gulf near the northwest corner of the Aegean Sea. It was one of the main sea ports in the provinces of Greece and Asia, and was accordingly considered a leading shipping and naval center. Thessalonica enjoyed another advantage. The Egnatian Way, the main Roman road from Rome to the Orient via Byzantium (modern Istanbul), passed right through the city. These factors put Thessalonica in direct contact with many other important cities by both land and sea. It is no wonder that this thriving metropolis achieved commercial dominance throughout this part of the world.

A famous woman immortalized

The historical roots of Thessalonica go back to 315 BC when Cassander built it near the site of an ancient city called Therma (named for the hot springs in the area). He chose this location because of its ideal proximity to other cities. After laying the foundation of the new city, he affectionately named it after his wife, Thanica, who was a half sister of Alexander the Great. Cassander was a Greek general under Alexander.

Many years later (around 168 BC), the Romans conquered the area and divided Macedonia into four districts. They named Thessalonica the capital of the second district. Still later, when the Romans made Macedonia a province in 146 BC, Thessalonica became the seat of provincial administration. Then in 42 BC, Thessalonica received the status of a free city from Anthony and Octavian (later called Caesar Augustus) because the Thessalonians had helped them defeat their adversaries, Brutus and Cassius. From this time forward, the Thessalonians were given the privilege of ruling themselves. They did this by means of five or six "politarchs" (city rulers), a senate, and a public assembly.

Paul: a transformed missionary

Paul was a missionary for much of his life, both before and after his conversion to Christianity. He was a Jew by birth, but his education was far from what a normal Jew would have received. His learning encompassed not only the Pharisaic approach to the Jewish law but also the Greek disciplines of rhetoric and classical literature. As a Pharisee, he believed that God had set him apart to study and live by the Torah (the law of Moses), and like a good Pharisee, he expected a Man to arise who would liberate Israel from the grip of Roman domination. Accordingly, when some Jews began saying that Jesus (who obviously hadn't overthrown Rome) was this predicted Messiah, he stood against them with a vengeance!

In a sense, Saul (Paul's Jewish name) became a zealous anti-Christian missionary. His first appearance in the New Testament is that of a persecutor of the church of Jesus Christ. He officiated at the stoning of Stephen; he imprisoned every Christian he could get his hands on in Jerusalem; and he even made "missionary trips" to areas outside of Palestine to bring back believers in Christ who had fled for safety (Acts 7:58–8:3, 9:1-2; 1 Corinthians 15:9; Philippians 3:6). His mission was to stop the spread of Christianity.

It was on such a trip to Damascus that Saul had a blinding encounter with Jesus Christ. This event, which took place around AD 35, led him to turn from Pharisaism to a devoted obedience to the living and resurrected Christ. He ended up joining those he had been persecuting! Formerly he was a missionary against the church of

Christ. Now he became a missionary par excellence for the cause of Christ.

After his conversion to Christianity, Paul engaged in three great missionary tours. His second missionary tour took place around AD 49 (about fourteen years after his conversion) and brought him to several important cities, including Philippi, Thessalonica, Corinth, and Ephesus.

Paul visits Thessalonica

Upon arriving in Thessalonica, Paul at once set himself to his usual activities of soul-winning and earning a livelihood. He found a friend in a certain Jason, who was apparently one of Paul's earliest converts in the city. Jason provided his home as a base of operations for Paul and his missionary companions. Once settled, Paul probably went to work immediately making tents to earn money as he had done in other cities, for later in his letters to the Thessalonians he reminded them that he had worked "night and day in order not to be a burden to anyone while we preached the gospel of God to you" (1 Thessalonians 2:9, 2 Thessalonians 3:8).

When the time came to preach the gospel, Paul followed his normal custom of first going to the local Jewish synagogue, where he knew he would find people who held a great deal in common with him: a mutual respect for the Old Testament, theological concepts, and cultural practices. In his thinking, this was where he stood the greatest chance for success.

As a trained teacher, Paul was allowed to speak in the synagogue. According to Luke, his main message to the Thessalonians consisted of two points: (1) the Old Testament taught a suffering, dying, and resurrected Messiah; and (2) these predictions were fulfilled in Jesus of Nazareth (Acts 1:7).

Paul's mission met with immediate success, and many believed, both Jews and Greeks. First Thessalonians 1:9 indicates that many of his Greek converts were former idol-worshipers. Most people in the ancient world worshiped natural forces and human drives, conceived of as gods who could be portrayed in wood, stone, or metal. Sexuality was a strong feature of pagan worship, and Paul found it necessary to address this very issue in 1 Thessalonians 4:1-8. The pursuit of religious ecstacy through sex was a hard habit to break.

The core of this young church was no doubt made up of "God-fearers," a Jewish term for Greeks who attached themselves in varying degrees to the Jewish worship and way of life without as yet becoming full converts. To become a full convert involved circumcision for males, but Greeks viewed this rite as a repugnant mutilation of the body. Paul's message included all of the attractive elements of Judaism without the unattractive ones.

These God-fearers were openly dissatisfied with pagan morality and were already drawn to Jewish ethical teaching. They were also impressed by Jewish monotheism. Yet in spite of their attraction to Judaism, they disliked its narrow nationalism and ritual requirements. Christianity did away with these objections, and provided a loftier concept of God as well as a nobler ethic centered in the person of Jesus Christ. Paul's Christ welcomed all races, in contrast to Jewish exclusivism. This group of Greeks provided Paul with fertile soil on which to plant the seeds of the gospel in this Thessalonian synagogue.

Persecution begins

Because many were converting from Judaism to Christianity, the Jewish leaders saw Paul's message as a serious threat. They hired troublemakers to spread false accusations about him and his associates. A mob ended up storming Jason's house. But failing to find the missionaries, the mob dragged Jason before the politarchs. Jason was charged with harboring treasonous revolutionaries. These revolutionaries were supposedly teaching the people to disobey Roman law and to follow a king other than Caesar.

The politarchs saw through the motives of these Jewish zealots and required only that Jason guarantee that the missionaries would not disturb the city's peace any longer. Paul and his friends chose to leave Thessalonica to avoid further trouble.

Paul's first letter to Thessalonica

Upon leaving Thessalonica, Paul, Silas, and Timothy proceeded about forty miles west along the Egnatian Way to Berea. They ministered in this area for a short time until some of the hostile Thessalonian Jews tracked them down and incited the Berean Jews to expel them from their city.

Paul accordingly headed for Athens while Silas and Timothy remained in Berea. After arriving in Athens, he immediately sent a message back to his companions in Berea asking them to join him, which they did (Acts 17:10-15, 1 Thessalonians 3:1-5).

When they met up again, Paul was so concerned about the Thessalonian converts that he decided to send Timothy back to Thessalonica in order to check on their welfare. The circumstances of his hasty departure had meant his new converts would be exposed to persecution for which they were scarcely prepared. Paul simply had not had sufficient time to give them all the basic teaching he thought they required.

After revisiting Thessalonica, Timothy rejoined Paul at his next stop, Corinth, with encouraging news (Acts 18:1,5; 1 Thessalonians 3:6-7). In spite of heavy persecution, the Thessalonians were standing strong in their new faith. But Timothy's report also indicated that they were experiencing some problems for which they needed instruction from Paul. They sent questions back to Paul via Timothy, and Paul responded by writing a letter to them from Corinth. The letter is simply addressed to "the church of the Thessalonians in God our Father and the Lord Jesus Christ."

1. Jacobs, *Anthology Graecae*, volume II, page 98, No. 14. Cited in *Archaeology and the New Testament*, by Merrill F. Unger (Grand Rapids, MI: Zondervan, 1962), page 226.
2. Strabo, volume VII, paragraphs 323 and 330. Compare Harold R. Willoughby, "Archaeology and Christian Beginnings," *Biblical Archaeology*, volume 3 (September 1939), pages 32-33. Cited in Unger, page 226.

Overview and 1 Thessalonians 1:1

To the Church

Before getting immersed in the details of Paul's words to the Thessalonians, take an overview of the whole letter. Get a feel for the "big picture." Potentially confusing verses will be clearer later if you can see how they fit into Paul's overall frame of thought.

The best preparation for understanding 1 Thessalonians is to read it several times in one sitting. Start by reading it once silently and then again aloud. Get a general impression of what Paul wants to accomplish.

First impressions

1. Would you say that this letter is more practical than doctrinal, or vice versa?

_____

_____

_____

2. Did you notice many personal references as you went through the letter? If so, what does this tell you about the nature of the letter?

_____

_____

_____

_____

3. a. Describe the mood of the letter. Is Paul exhorting, comforting, describing, giving direction, persuading, warning?

_____

_____

_____

b. Are there any mood changes in the letter? If so, where?

_____

_____

_____

_____

4. a. Repetition is a clue to the ideas and concepts a writer considers most important to his message. What words or concepts occur over and over again in this letter?

_____

_____

_____

_____

b. What hints does this give you as to the main focus of Paul's argument?

_____

_____

_____

_____

Broad outline

5. Reread the entire letter, preferably using a different translation than the one you've been using. This time, describe each main section of the letter with a

14

short sentence. Or—as an option—choose a title
to describe each main section.

1:1 _____

1:2-10 _____

2:1-16 _____

2:17–3:5 _____

3:6-13 _____

4:1-12 _____

4:13-18 _____

5:1-11 _____

5:12-15 _____

5:16-24 _____

5:25-28 _____

Theme/purpose

6. What does the content of 1 Thessalonians suggest
   Paul wanted to accomplish with his readers?

   _____

   _____

   _____

   _____

   _____

7. Test your ability to refine by stating the main message or theme of 1 Thessalonians in one sentence.

   _____

   _____

   _____

8. What are some of the different subjects Paul discusses in supporting his main theme?

_____

_____

_____

_____

_____

9. If you have not already done so, read the historical background on pages 9-12 of this guide. Is there any information that seems particularly helpful to you in understanding Paul's letter to the Thessalonians? Please explain briefly.

_____

_____

_____

_____

10. Based on what you have discovered so far, assign a title to Paul's letter to the Thessalonians.

_____

_____

Study Skill—Bible Study Aids
If you would like to study the background of
1 Thessalonians in greater detail, consult one
of the sources listed on pages 105-107. These
and similar commentaries will also be quite
helpful if you decide to study another book of
the Bible on your own.

Greetings

Grace and peace (1:1). Among the early Greeks, *grace* was a common salutation and greeting. The word *peace* served the same purpose for the Jews. Paul thus combines Greek and Hebrew salutations and attaches theological significance to them. In Paul's theology, grace signified God's unmerited favor toward humans.

---

11. a. The letter begins, "Paul, Silas and Timothy: To the church of the Thessalonians . . ." (1:1). What indications do you see in 2:18, 3:5, and 5:27 that Paul actually wrote (or dictated) the letter?

_____

_____

_____

_____

b. If Paul was the author, why do you think he began the letter the way he did?

_____

_____

_____

_____

12. Consider the order in which Paul uses the terms *grace* and *peace*. How is one the foundation of the other?

_____

_____

_____

_____

13. Is there any part of this lesson that specifically touches upon an area of your life and moves you to respond in some way? If so, write down your insight here, along with how you want to respond.

_____

_____

_____

For Thought and Discussion: What does the small word "in" (1:1) suggest to you about the Thessalonians' spiritual standing before God?

_____

_____

_____

_____

14. In your initial readings of 1 Thessalonians, you may
   have come across difficult concepts that you would
   like clarified or questions you would like answered
   as you go deeper into this study. While your
   thoughts are still fresh, you may want to jot down
   your questions here to serve as a "personal objec-
   tive log" for your investigation of this letter.

_____

_____

_____

_____

_____

For the group

Unless you have already become acquainted with other
members in your group, you might want to spend
some time in your next few meetings establishing
trust, common ground, and a sense of where each person is coming from. This should enable you to be more
frank when discussing how 1 Thessalonians personally
applies to you later on. At this first meeting, share
something of your past with the group—for example,
what you remember about first becoming a Christian.
Or you might want to discuss your responses to question 13. This will help to show each other how you see
yourselves. It might also be helpful to talk about what
each of your personal goals are in regard to what you
want to get out of this study of 1 Thessalonians.

   Compare your sentence summaries (in question
5) with those in the following chart. There is no single
correct answer, so discuss why you prefer one sentence
summary to another. Any group members who felt

successful with question 7 may want to share with the rest of the group how they went about summarizing main themes.

Chart of First Thessalonians: Paul's Purpose

Paul writes to answer certain ethical, doctrinal, and practical questions the Thessalonians have, as well as to commend their faith, exhort young converts, and answer false charges made against him by unbelieving Jews.

1:1	Paul greets the saints in Thessalonica.
1:2-10	Paul gives thanks for the faith of the Thessalonians.
2:1-16	Paul defends his ministry in Thessalonica.
2:17–3:5	Paul expresses his desire to see the Thessalonians.
3:6-13	Paul is happy about Timothy's encouraging report.
4:1-12	Paul urges the Thessalonians to live to please God.
4:13-18	Paul instructs them about the coming of the Lord.
5:1-11	Paul urges them to be ready for the coming of the Lord.
5:12-15	Paul gives instructions about life in the church.
5:16-24	Paul exhorts the Thessalonians to holy living.
5:25-28	Paul closes.

1 Thessalonians 1:2-10

Thanksgiving

Briefly read through Acts 17:1-9 as a backdrop for this study. It is a mini-history of Paul's visit to Thessalonica.

The Thessalonians had less than a year of Christian experience. They were immature and were facing many difficulties and persecutions. Yet despite their circumstances, they were constantly displaying abundant faith, love, and hope in their daily lives. Their faithfulness to God in the midst of affliction had even attained for them a measure of fame!

1. Read 1 Thessalonians 1:2-10, preferably once silently and once aloud. What do you think Paul's purpose was in saying these things to the Thessalonians? What effect in the hearts of his hearers do you think Paul wanted to produce?

_____

_____

_____

_____

Study Skill—Christian Doctrine
Christians of all denominations agree that God is a Trinity. That is, there is only one God, but in the unity of the Godhead there are three eternal
(continued on page 22)

(continued from page 21)
and coequal Persons: the Father, the Son, and
the Holy Spirit. However, this doctrine was not
formally stated until the fourth century AD, and
the word *Trinity* is not in the Bible. Is it, then, a
biblical concept? We'd need to study more than
just 1 Thessalonians to decide, but it is a good
idea when studying a book to keep alert for
statements that affirm or refute doctrines we've
been taught. Biblical passages can flesh out
and clarify dry doctrines, and we may find our-
selves changing our minds about aspects of
some doctrines.

2. a. Read 1:2-10, and trace the role of each Person of
the Trinity in the lives of the Thessalonians.
(Keep in mind that the word *God* generally refers
to the Father and the word *Lord* generally refers
to Jesus Christ.) Write down what Paul says in
these verses about . . .

The Father _____

_____

_____

_____

_____

The Son _____

_____

_____

_____

_____

The Holy Spirit _____

_____

_____

_____

_____

22

b. What do these observations tell you about each
of the following?

The Father _____

_____

_____

_____

_____

The Son _____

_____

_____

_____

_____

The Holy Spirit _____

_____

_____

_____

_____

c. What do you think is Paul's purpose in mention-
ing the Father, Son, and Spirit so often in these
verses?

_____

_____

_____

_____

Study Skill—Cross References
Other parts of Scripture often shed light on a
passage you are studying. These are called
"cross-references."

For Further Study:
Trace the triad of faith, hope, and love through the New Testament:
Romans 5:1-5;
1 Corinthians 13:13;
Galatians 5:5-6;
Colossians 1:3-5;
1 Thessalonians 5:8;
Hebrews 6:10-12,
10:22-24; 1 Peter
1:3-9,21-22. Why do you think this triad occurs so often in Scripture? Make a list of how these three characteristics are outwardly manifested in each of the passages above.

Work produced by faith (1:3). Work springing out of faith or, rather, belonging to faith, and therefore characterizing it—your faith's work. Faith always produces action in the life of the believer. (Take a look at Romans 1:5, Galatians 5:6, 2 Thessalonians 1:11, and James 2:14-26 as cross-references.)

Endurance (1:3). Literally "bearing up patiently under a heavy load." The Thessalonians' ability to bear up under a heavy load was based on their hope in the Lord Jesus Christ.

3. What three characteristics does Paul mention as being true of the Thessalonians in 1:3?

4. Read Paul's description of love in 1 Corinthians 13:4-8. What actions might Paul be referring to when he writes of "labor prompted by love" (1 Thessalonians 1:3)?

5. a. In practical terms, what does it mean to hope in Christ?

b. How does the "endurance" aspect of this hope manifest itself in 1:6-10?

Chosen (1:4). This is a difficult concept. Both the Old Testament and the New Testament indicate that God has chosen to bless some individuals with eternal life (e.g., Deuteronomy 4:37, 7:6-7; Isaiah 44:1-2; Romans 9; Ephesians 1:4-6,11; Colossians 3:12; 2 Thessalonians 2:13). It is equally clear that each individual is personally responsible before God for his or her decision to trust (or not to trust) in Jesus Christ (John 3, Romans 5). In fact, the prophets (Amos 3:2, for instance) stress that God's chosen people have even more responsibility than those whom He has not chosen.

It is not easy to understand how divine election and human responsibility can both be true. That both are true is clear from Scripture. How they can both be true is incomprehensible to finite minds.

For Thought and Discussion: Has your hope in Christ affected the way you respond to hard times? Explain.

For Thought and Discussion: How do you know God has chosen you, personally?

6. What does 1:4-10 reveal about the basis of Paul's assurance of the Thessalonians' salvation? How did Paul know that they were "chosen"?

_____

_____

_____

_____

7. In light of Paul's previous life as a proud Pharisee, what significance do you see in his calling a largely Gentile group "brothers" in 1:4?

_____

_____

_____

8. a. Take a look at Paul's description of the "gospel" in 1 Corinthians 15:1-8. What do you think Paul means by "our gospel" in 1 Thessalonians 1:5?

_____

_____

25

For Further Study: For more on how the gospel "comes with power" and the Holy Spirit, take a look at Romans 1:16; 15:13,18-19; and 1 Corinthians 2:4-5.

For Further Study: Paul says a lot about imitation in the New Testament. For more on this important aspect of spirituality, see 1 Corinthians 4:6, 11:1; 1 Thessalonians 2:14; 2 Thessalonians 3:7,9; and 1 Timothy 4:12.

_____

_____

b. What do you think he means in this verse when he says that this gospel came "with power"?

_____

_____

_____

_____

Suffering (1:6). The Jewish converts in the church were hated and persecuted by the unbelieving Jews of the synagogue who were extremely antagonistic to the gospel of Jesus. The Gentile converts suffered in the sense that they had to swim against the swift current of idolatry that flowed like a torrent through commercial Thessalonica.

9. a. How is it possible to have joy even when following Christ leads to suffering, as Paul says in 1:6?

_____

_____

_____

_____

b. How is joy related to imitating Christ (1:6)?

_____

_____

_____

_____

Rang out (1:8). Has the idea of "reverberated." Paul sees the Thessalonians as relay stations or amplifiers that not only received the gospel message but sent it farther on its way with even greater power and scope. Like a public address system, Paul's words were repeated by many different "speakers" throughout the various provinces.

10. The Thessalonians "reverberated" the Lord's message, and Paul informs them that "your faith in God has become known everywhere" (1:8). Compare this reference to "your faith" in verse 8 with the reference to faith in 1:3. What relationship do you see between the two?

_____

_____

_____

_____

Study Skill—Summarizing
Test your skills at refining by summarizing the "gist" of 1:6-8 in one sentence.

Turned (verse 9). The Greek word is in the aorist tense, which indicates that they turned from idolatry once for all. It was a single, definite act, a deliberate choice to turn to God from idolatry.

11. Paul says in 1:9 that the Thessalonians turned from idols to serve the living and true God. What is Paul telling us about idols (via contrast) in this statement?

_____

_____

_____

_____

Wrath (1:10). God's wrath is poured out on unrighteous people because of their refusal to trust in Christ

Optional Application: According to Paul, the things that should make Christians stand out are faith, hope, love, joy despite suffering, and a refusal to worship idols. Even as brand-new believers, the Thessalonians were already becoming known for these qualities. What about you? What are you known for? How can you become known for hope or love?

For Thought and Discusion: a. In Ephesians 5:5 and Colossians 3:5, Paul states that greed is a form of idolatry. Why is that?
  b. When you think of a greedy person, what picture comes to mind? Is it possible for nice, middle-class Christians to be greedy? What would be the signs?

Optional Application: Do you have any idols? What about money, security, your career, your image, your ministry, your home, your car, your clothes, your appearance? How would a person know when he or she has made something an idol?

27

For Further Study:
On a Bible map, locate some of the cities and provinces mentioned in 1 Thessalonians. Notice how Greece was once divided into two major provinces: Macedonia and Achaia (1:7-8). Find Thessalonica, and notice how it is ideally located on the gulf of the Aegean Sea, and how it lies in proximity with other major cities.

On Paul's second missionary tour, he visited such major cities as Tarsus, Philippi, Thessalonica, Berea, Athens, Corinth, and Ephesus. Get a feel for the layout of the land so that your reading will come alive as you encounter some of these locations in 1 Thessalonians.

(John 3:36, Romans 1:18). Some scholars believe "the coming wrath" refers to a specific future time period known as the "tribulation period" (compare Jeremiah 30:4-7 and Revelation 6–18).

---

12. a. In Genesis 6, God rescues Noah and his family before He sends the flood to destroy rebel humans. In Genesis 19:1-29, God rescues Lot before destroying Sodom and Gomorrah. What does it say about God that He rescues His people before sending wrath?

_____

_____

_____

_____

b. So why doesn't God rescue us from all suffering? What insights on this does 1 Thessalonians 1:2-10 offer?

_____

_____

_____

_____

_____

Study Skill—Outlining
You can help assure that you understand a passage by outlining it. State each central teaching in 1:2-10 as a sentence. Then list any subpoints.

Your response

The last step of Bible study is asking yourself, "What difference does the passage make to my life? How should it cause me to think or act?" Applications require time, thought, prayer, and sometimes even discussion with another person. Question 13 focuses on the Thessalonian believers as an example of how we should live as Christians.

13. a. How do you see the Thessalonians as examples for your daily living?

_____

_____

_____

_____

b. Where do you fall short?

_____

_____

_____

c. What do you suppose people think of when they pray for you?

_____

_____

_____

_____

Optional Application:
Do people see in your life the evidence that the Word of God has come in power, and that you have been noticeably transformed?

Optional Application:
How is Paul an example to you in thanksgiving and prayer (1:2-3)? (*Optional*: Look up Psalm 95:2, 100:4; Philippians 4:6; and 1 Thessalonians 5:18 as cross-references.)

Optional Application:
Is there any area of sin in your life where you need to follow the Thessalonians' example by turning from it once for all and turning to God with all your heart?

For the group

We cannot see the wind, but we can see the effects of the wind (the leaves blowing to and fro, etc.). Similarly, it is impossible to see faith, love, or hope; they are immaterial things. But they can be manifested in a very definite and noticeable way.

Discuss the manifestations of this scriptural triad in the lives of the Thessalonian believers. Then discuss this triad in relation to your own lives. What changes can you make in your lives as a result of understanding this passage?

LESSON THREE

1 Thessalonians 2:1-16

Paul's Ministry

Paul's enemies in Thessalonica were ruthless! Apparently, they had committed themselves to spreading slanderous rumors about his life, motives, and methods in his gospel campaign, and they were relentless in their efforts.

Their primary accusation seems to be that Paul was more interested in making money out of his converts than in presenting true teaching. The accusation would have been easy because there were many itinerant preachers in the Roman Empire who desired only to feather their own nests. Paul's enemies were representing him as being nothing more than another low-class preaching vagrant.

In the present passage, Paul called the Thessalonians to the witness stand to demonstrate two crucial things. First, Paul demonstrated he had confidence in them. He knew they would not succumb to the propaganda. And second, he demonstrated that all the facts needed for his vindication were common knowledge. No one had to search for material to prove his innocence. An accusation of insincerity could hardly stand in the light of such public knowledge of Paul and his great accomplishments in Thessalonica.

Read through the whole passage at least once before beginning to answer the questions. You may also want to skim through the questions in this lesson before you start answering any.

Paul's ministry in Thessalonica

1. Most of 2:1-16 is about Paul and his ministry. How does this compare with chapter 1?

_____

_____

_____

_____

2. Read 2:1 and compare it with 1:4-10. How was Paul's visit to Thessalonica not a failure according to these verses?

_____

_____

_____

_____

We dared (2:2). Literally "we waxed bold in our God. . . ." Refers to boldness in the sense of speaking out publicly. It denotes a state of mind where words flow freely, an attitude of feeling "at home" with no sense of stress or strain. No matter what his outward circumstances were, Paul always felt at home because he lived "in Christ" (Ephesians 1:3) and in God (Acts 17:28).

Opposition (2:2). Ancient Greeks used this word for the rigors and strains characteristic of athletic contests. The English word *agony* is derived from the Greek form of this word.

3. a. It is clear that Paul was deeply hurt by his treatment in Philippi (2:2). Read through Acts 16:11-40 and summarize the suffering Paul had to endure in this city.

_____

_____

_____

_____

_____

_____

b. Why didn't Paul and his companions let such
suffering stop them (1 Thessalonians 2:2)?

_____

_____

_____

_____

Error or impure motives (2:3). Paul's enemies had
accused him of being completely mistaken in his
preaching. He was also accused of seeking his own
honor and not God's, as well as being a "preacher
for profit."

Trick (2:3). The Greeks used this word to describe a
lure for catching fish. It eventually came to depict
any type of cunning used for profit. There were all
kinds of wandering teachers during the first century who resorted to various gimmicks to attract
people and get their money. This is what Paul had
been accused of by his enemies.

Approved (2:4). This word literally means "shown by
testing to be genuine." The tense of the Greek verb
indicates not only a past approval, but a continuing one. "We stand approved . . ." is the sense of it.

Greed (2:5). This is derived from two Greek words
meaning "to have" and "more." It refers to self-
interest in the broadest sense.

Praise from men (2:6). Traveling philosophers and
public orators were common in the Roman
Empire. They spoke from city to city, entertaining
and seeking as large a personal following as possible. The goal was twofold: fame (with its accom-
panying praise) and fortune. Paul had apparently
been accused of seeking such praise in his ministry to the Thessalonians.

**For Thought and
Discussion:** Relate 2:3
to the mention of "his
gospel" in 2:2. How do
these verses indicate
that Paul's appeal could
not spring from error,
impure motives, or
trickery?

For Further Study:
For more on Paul being
"entrusted with the
gospel," take a look at
1 Corinthians 9:17,
Galatians 2:7-8, and
Titus 1:1-3. As you go
through these passages,
keep in mind that the
underlying meaning of
"entrust" is to "act as a
house manager" or
"steward." Paul was a
house manager or
steward of the gospel.

33

4. a. Summarize in your own words the accusations Paul was likely answering in 2:4-6.

_____

_____

_____

_____

_____

   b. What was Paul's approach in refuting the slander of his enemies in these verses? What evidence does he cite?

_____

_____

_____

_____

5. What metaphor does Paul use to describe his relationship with the Thessalonians in 2:7? What do you think he wants to get across by using this image?

_____

_____

_____

_____

_____

_____

6. a. What two things does Paul say he and his companions were delighted to do because of their love for the Thessalonians (2:8)?

_____

_____

_____

b. What do you think was involved in sharing "our lives as well" (2:8)?

_____

_____

_____

_____

For Thought and Discussion: The word Paul uses for "love" (2:8) is *agape*, which refers to a self-giving and self-sacrificial kind of love. Discuss the significance of this kind of love, and contrast it with what often passes for love in modern times.

Preached (2:9). Signifies the action of a herald. A herald simply passes on words given to him. He does not devise a message of his own or even elaborate on the message given to him. Paul considers himself a herald, passing on "the gospel of God" to the Thessalonians.

Work (2:9). Paul was a "tentmaker" (Acts 18:3). Most Roman tents were made of leather, so chances are that Paul did other kinds of leatherwork as well.

7. a. Why was it so important to Paul that he supported himself financially, rather than living off donations from the Thessalonians? Compare 2 Thessalonians 3:7-12.

_____

_____

_____

_____

b. In view of the fact that Paul had the right to be financially supported by the Thessalonians if he so chose (1 Thessalonians 2:6), what does 2:9 reveal to you about Paul and his attitude toward the Thessalonians?

_____

_____

_____

_____

35

8. What is Paul's point in 2:10?

_____

_____

_____

_____

Kingdom (2:12). The New Testament refers to a present aspect of the Kingdom (Romans 14:17, 1 Corinthians 4:20, Colossians 1:13) as well as a future aspect of the Kingdom (Matthew 25:34; Acts 14:22; 1 Corinthians 6:9-10, 15:50). Since Paul associates "kingdom" with "glory" in this passage, it seems likely that he is thinking here of the future aspect of the Kingdom of God. In any event, both aspects involve a recognition of God's righteous rule operating within people and over people.

---

9. a. In verses 11-12, Paul uses the metaphor of "father" to describe his relationship to the Thessalonians. What are some of the fatherly activities Paul engaged in with the Thessalonians?

_____

_____

_____

b. How does this image of spiritual fathering build on Paul's description of spiritual mothering in 2:7? What does it add?

_____

_____

_____

_____

c. In your opinion, what is the significance of Paul describing his relationship to the Thessalonians as parent-child rather than, say, teacher-student or commander-soldier?

_____

_____

_____

_____

For Thought and Discussion: Can you imagine being a spiritual parent, helping someone else grow in Christ? What attracts or scares you about the prospect?

10. Have you ever had a spiritual parent who cared for you, encouraged you, etc., in your spiritual growth? If so, how has that affected you? If not, how might your life have been different if you had had such a person?

_____

_____

_____

_____

_____

For Thought and Discussion: How do Paul's words in 2:13 indicate an intrinsic authority in what he says (as opposed to what the traveling philosophers say)?

11. What do you think Paul means when he says the word of God "is at work in you who believe" (2:13)? (What is the word at work doing? How can a word be at work doing anything?)

_____

_____

_____

_____

_____

12. How did the Thessalonians become "imitators" of God's churches in Judea (2:14)?

_____

_____

_____

37

For Further Study:
In 2:14 Paul tells the Thessalonians he recognizes that "you suffered from your own countrymen." Apparently, immediately following Paul's initial visit to Thessalonica, the persecution instigated by the Jewish leaders was carried out by Gentiles. Acts 17:5-9 is a mini-history of this event. Read this passage and summarize what happened.

For Further Study:
Continue constructing the outline you began in lesson 2. Let your main divisions be 2:1-6, 2:7-9, 2:10-12, and 2:13-16. (If you persist in your outlining efforts, you will finish this study with a complete outline of 1 Thessalonians.)

Heap up their sins to the limit (2:16). It seems that because of His righteous nature, God will only allow an individual or a group of individuals to accumulate so much sin, and then He judges that sin. Genesis 15:16 suggests God does not exercise such judgment before this limit has been reached (which He alone knows). Those persecuting the Thessalonians were hastening God's judgment on themselves because of their actions. A cross-reference for this idea is Matthew 23:29-32.

Wrath (2:16). This "wrath" has been interpreted in four ways: (1) It may refer to what was the coming destruction of Jerusalem in AD 70. If Paul had prophetic insight that this would happen in just twenty years, he could have spoken of it as already present because of its absolute certainty. (2) It may refer to God's turning away from the Jews in order to create for Himself a unique body of believers made up of both Jews and Gentiles. (3) It may refer to God's general wrath that is upon all who fail to believe in Christ (John 3:36). (4) It may refer to the future tribulation period in which God will judge unbelieving Jews (Jeremiah 30:7).

13. Christians tend to believe that God's blessing has departed from them if they are suffering some form of persecution. How does 1 Thessalonians 2:14-16 counter this kind of thinking?

_____

_____

_____

_____

_____

_____

_____

Study Skill—Summarizing
In your own words, summarize the content of 2:1-16. Focus only on the big ideas.

Your response

14. a. What have you learned from 2:1-16 that seems relevant to you personally right now?

_____

_____

_____

_____

b. Is there anything you'd like to do about this? What?

_____

_____

_____

_____

15. List any questions you have about this passage.

_____

_____

_____

Teachers and Trades

"Teachers and Trades" was a Jewish custom, based on the rabbis' teaching that every boy should learn a trade. This was a matter of sheer economic necessity: there were no paid teachers in Palestine. Accordingly, it was necessary for a rabbi (or teacher) to have some other means of income than the small gifts that might now and then be made to him. Even boys from wealthy families were taught a trade.

From Acts 18:3, we learn that Paul's particular trade was tentmaking. Based on 1 Thessalonians 2:9

(continued on page 40)

Optional Application: Can you think of any occasions in the past year where you resisted sharing the gospel with someone because of fear or embarrassment? If so, what practical steps can you take to imitate Paul in his daring (2:2) while speaking to others about the gospel?

For Thought and Discussion: Malicious rumors were circulating about Paul. How did he handle them? What application can you draw from this in regard to how you should respond to people who speak evil of you?

Optional Application: What would it look like this week for you to "live lives worthy of God" (2:12)?

Optional Application: Spend a few moments and meditate on your glorious eternal future with God (2:12). Then examine your present lifestyle. Are there any changes you are motivated to make in view of your eternal destiny?

(continued from page 39)
and 2 Thessalonians 3:7-12, it would seem that Paul arose before dawn and continued on after dusk to earn money by his trade. He did this so that he would not be a financial burden to the Christians in Thessalonica. He also did this to draw a clear distinction between himself and the money-hungry itinerant philosophers who were so common in the Roman Empire.

For the group

Divide the group into two "Think Tanks." Each Think Tank will deal with a specific issue for five or ten minutes and then share the results with the whole group.

Think Tank One: Make a list of "negatives" found in 2:3-6 that should not characterize a Christian worker. Then discuss your answers to the following questions:

- Do you see any of these characteristics cropping up from time to time in Christian ministries?
- What would you say is the root problem that needs to be dealt with in overcoming such characteristics?
- What preventive steps can you take today to ensure that such characteristics will never be a part of your own personal ministry to others?

Think Tank Two: Make a list of "positives" found in 2:7-11 that should characterize a Christian worker. Then discuss your answers to the following questions:

- Do you see these characteristics in the ministries you are familiar with?
- What would you say is the spiritual key to manifesting such characteristics consistently in Christian work?
- What steps can you take today to foster the development of such characteristics in your own personal ministry to others?

Allow a few minutes for each Think Tank to share its findings with the whole group. Following this, close with a time of prayer for the ministries you are familiar with as well as your own personal ministries. Be specific in your requests to God for yourselves.

1 Thessalonians 2:17–3:5

Paul's Desire

As always, start your own study by reading through 1 Thessalonians 2:17–3:5 several times. Pay special attention to the personal relationships you see in this passage.

As you go through 2:17–3:5, keep in mind that Paul's enemies accused him of many things, among these the suggestion that he had no intention of revisiting Thessalonica. His continued absence from them, they argued, was proof that he had no real concern for his converts. One of Paul's goals in this passage is to answer such accusations.

Paul desires to see the Thessalonians

Torn away (2:17). Literally "to be orphaned." Paul felt as though his family was being torn apart when he left them. Paul likened himself to a mother (2:7), a father (2:11), and now an orphan.

1. First Thessalonians 2:17 indicates that Paul and his companions were "torn away" from the Thessalonians. Review how this occurred by reading Acts 17:5-10, and briefly summarize the event here.

_____

_____

_____

41

For Further Study: You can also read about Paul's arrival in Athens in Acts 17:14-15, and then his arrival in Corinth in Acts 18:1-17. It was during his stay in Corinth that Paul wrote this epistle to the Thessalonians.

For Thought and Discussion: How do you think Satan stopped Paul from returning to Thessalonica? What do you think he means in 1 Thessalonians 2:18?

Optional Application: Who will be your glory, your sign of victory in Christ, when Christ returns? Have you affected anyone's life in the way Paul affected the Thessalonians so significantly?

_____

_____

_____

Stopped (2:18). The verb literally means "to cut into." This word was used among the Greeks to refer to cutting up a road in order to make it impassable. In popular usage it came to mean "hinder" by any means available.

_____

2. Acts 17:5-9 indicates that many unbelieving Jews rose up against Paul when he visited Thessalonica. However, these angry Jews were not all that Paul had to contend with. What does 1 Thessalonians 2:18 tell you about Paul's opposition from the spiritual realm?

_____

_____

_____

_____

_____

Paul's future crown (2:19). Commonly denoted a laurel wreath awarded to the victor at Greek games.

Comes (2:19). The Greeks often used this word to refer to the arrival of a great personage or even royalty, such as an emperor or a king. In the New Testament, it became a technical expression for the royal visit *par excellence*, the Second Coming of the Lord Jesus Christ.

_____

3. a. Satan was able temporarily to stand in the way of Paul's plans to see the Thessalonians (2:18). In spite of Satan's momentary success, what do verses 19 and 20 indicate about the ultimate victory that awaited Paul?

_____

_____

_____

_____

_____

_____

b. What does Paul say will be his victory crown at the Second Coming of the Lord (2:19-20)?

_____

_____

_____

c. How does Paul express his feelings for the Thessalonians in this passage?

_____

_____

_____

d. How do you think it might have affected the Thessalonians to have Paul tell them this in the midst of their struggles?

_____

_____

_____

_____

Timothy is sent

4. a. What phrase occurs in 3:1 and again in 3:5 that indicates Paul's tremendous concern for the Thessalonians?

_____

_____

_____

For Further Study:
For more on the topic of crowns as rewards, take a look at 1 Corinthians 9:25; 2 Timothy 4:8; James 1:12; 1 Peter 5:4; Revelation 2:10, 4:10. Summarize what a Christian must do to earn such crowns. How do you think the earning of crowns relates to the offer of salvation by grace? Is it a contradiction? Explain.

43

For Thought and Discussion: How do you think first-century Christians would evaluate modern Christians in regard to our willingness to render service?

b. Why do you suppose Paul felt that strongly?

_____

_____

_____

_____

_____

Strengthen (3:2). Carries the idea of making firm or solid. This word was often used of erecting a buttress to shore up or provide support for a building.

Encourage (3:2). Carries the idea "to call to the side of." It portrays one person standing alongside another in order to put courage into them. Timothy was standing alongside the Thessalonians and encouraging them in their difficulty.

5. Why do you suppose Paul made such a point of underscoring Timothy's status both as a brother and even "God's fellow worker"?

_____

_____

_____

_____

_____

_____

Worker (3:2). When Paul referred to Timothy as God's fellow "worker," he chose a word that the Greeks used to denote the service of a table waiter. The word eventually came to signify lowly service of any kind. The early Christians adopted this word to give expression to the service that they were to render habitually to both God and man. Christianity without service was inconceivable to the first-century Christians.

6. What three purposes can you find in 3:2,5 for Paul's sending young Timothy to visit the Thessalonians?

_____

_____

_____

_____

_____

_____

Unsettled (3:3). The original meaning of this word among the Greeks had to do with a dog wagging its tail. In the present context it pictures the Thessalonians going back and forth because of their persecutions.

Destined (3:3). This is a strong verb meaning "appointed" and carrying the idea of "that which cannot be altered."

7. a. What can a strengthened faith prevent, according to 3:3?

_____

_____

_____

b. What can a strengthened faith not prevent?

_____

_____

_____

8. Read 3:3-5. Summarize as precisely as you can what Paul's concern was for the Thessalonians.

_____

_____

45

_____

_____

_____

9. Paul states in 3:3 that Christians are "destined" for trials. This is a difficult concept.

a. What constructive uses for trials are mentioned in these passages?

Psalm 119:67,71,75 _____

_____

_____

_____

Acts 11:19-21 _____

_____

_____

_____

Romans 5:3-4 _____

_____

_____

_____

2 Corinthians 4:7-12 _____

_____

_____

_____

2 Corinthians 4:17-18 _____

_____

_____

_____

b. From what you've read, what do you think Paul means by "destined"? Is it that God specifically sends each trial that comes our way, or that it's inevitable—given the radical nature of the gospel and the fallenness of the world—that we who follow Christ will get in trouble for it? Why do you think that?

_____

_____

_____

_____

_____

_____

For Further Study:
For more on the necessity of faith in spiritual survival, read through the various examples of faith found in Hebrews 11. Pay special attention to the various obstacles that different men and women of God faced and how faith enabled them to overcome these obstacles.

10. What do you believe was Paul's purpose in continually reminding the Thessalonians that persecution was an unavoidable certainty?

_____

_____

_____

_____

_____

11. Paul sent Timothy to find out how the Thessalonians' faith was holding up in the face of severe persecution (3:5). Why does persecution sometimes make faith falter?

_____

_____

_____

_____

_____

_____

47

For Further Study:
Scripture has quite a bit to say about Satan's rise as a tempter. Genesis 3, Matthew 4:1-11, and 1 Corinthians 7:5 are excellent references. That Christ Himself was tempted by Satan in Matthew 4:1-11 has a practical application for us. Read Hebrews 4:15-16, and state this application in the form of a principle.

Optional Application:
In what areas does the Tempter tempt you to falter in your faith?

Optional Application:
Paul ministered to the Thessalonians in absentia, and his ministry was extremely effective. Can you think of someone who lives far from you to whom you can spiritually minister today—by prayer, a phone call, writing a letter, or any other ways?

Optional Application:
Timothy ministered to the Thessalonians in person. Are you aware of anyone whose faith is in need of strengthening and encouraging? If so, decide on some specific steps you will take in order to imitate Timothy in his ministry.

12. What is the significance of Paul referring to Satan as the "tempter" in 3:5?

_____

_____

_____

_____

13. What sobering possibility is suggested in the words "our efforts might have been useless" (3:5)?

_____

_____

_____

_____

Your response

14. How is 1 Thessalonians 2:17–3:5 relevant to your life today?

_____

_____

_____

_____

_____

15. Is there anything you would like to do in response to what you've studied? Explain.

_____

_____

_____

_____

16. List any questions you have about this passage.

_____

_____

_____

_____

For the group

Paul considered the various "crowns" he might receive when Christ returns as a motivation for holy living. Discuss the question: Do you take such future rewards seriously in regard to your present lifestyle? If not, discuss the wisdom of following Paul's example of "taking the long look" (i.e., maintaining an eternal perspective in the course of daily living). What's hard about doing that? How would you cultivate an eternal perspective?

1 Thessalonians 3:6-13

Good News from Timothy

Timothy's encouraging report

1. Read 3:6-13 a couple of times. What is the general tone of this passage?

_____

_____

_____

_____

2. How does it compare with the tone of 2:17–3:5?

_____

_____

_____

_____

3. What is the significance of beginning this section with the word *but*?

_____

_____

_____

_____

Optional Application:
What news would
someone report about
your faith and love?

For Thought and
Discussion: What
specific manifestations
of faith may Paul have
been referring to in 3:7?
(See 1:3,6-10 and
2:13.)

Good news (3:6). This is the only place in the New
   Testament where Paul uses this specific Greek
   word for anything other than the gospel. That Paul
   uses it this once in regard to the report on the
   Thessalonians from Timothy is a reflection of the
   tremendous measure of joy it had brought him.

Faith and love (3:6). Paul has in mind the Thessalonians' relationships with both God and man. One is
   a *vertical* relationship, the other *horizontal*.

4. Why do you think faith and love are so important
   to Paul's message, in view of the Thessalonians' circumstances?

   _____

   _____

   _____

   _____

   _____

5. Did the Thessalonians believe the accusations
   Paul's enemies made against him? What evidence
   do you see in 3:6?

   _____

   _____

   _____

   _____

   _____

Really live (3:8). The opposition, unbelief, peril, and
   disappointment had so preyed upon Paul and his
   companions that they felt enveloped in the
   shadow of death. But Timothy's news from Thessalonica so revived him that it lifted him out of his
   gloom and, in a figurative sense, enabled him to
   "really live." His soul was so joyful over the stability of his spiritual children that he felt rejuvinated.

6. What did Paul mean when he acknowledged that the Thessalonians were "standing firm in the Lord" (3:8)?

_____

_____

_____

_____

7. Instead of taking credit for the Thessalonians' behavior, Paul thanked God for their behavior (3:9). Why do you think he did that?

_____

_____

_____

_____

For Thought and Discussion: Why do you suppose Paul felt his spiritual children's faith was a matter of his own life and death? Why was it so important to him?

Optional Application: Does helping someone come to faith or grow in faith give you the kind of charge it gave Paul? Why do you suppose that's so?

For Thought and Discussion: Paul was certainly a believer in frequent and continuous prayer (1:2-3, 3:10). Why is persistence in prayer so important?

Night and day (3:10). This refers not to prayer at two different times but to frequent prayer.

Supply (3:10). Among the ancient Greeks, this word was used to describe the setting of a broken bone, the equipping of an army, the outfitting of a fleet of ships for battle, and the mending of torn nets.

8. Why do you suppose it was so important to Paul that he get back to Thessalonica (3:10)?

_____

_____

_____

_____

Paul's prayer

Holy ones (3:13). This could equally be translated, "saints." To Paul, a saint was any Christian, since

53

For Further Study: Paul often breaks into prayer in the middle of a letter. Good examples of this include Ephesians 1:15-23, 3:14-21; Philippians 1:9-11; and Colossians 1:9-12.

all were holy to God. In the present context, "holy ones" may include departed saints, angels, or both.

9. Paul asks God for three things in 3:11-13. List these and state the relevance of each request in light of what the Thessalonians were dealing with.

3:11 _____

_____

_____

_____

_____

_____

3:12 _____

_____

_____

_____

_____

_____

3:13 _____

_____

_____

_____

_____

10. a. Paul prays that the Thessalonians' love would increase (3:12). Who might Paul be referring to when he says "everyone else"?

_____

_____

_____

b. Why was loving those people so important?

_____

_____

_____

_____

11. So far, Paul has closed every chapter in 1 Thessalonians with a reference to Christ's return (1:10, 2:19,
3:13). What do you think was his purpose in doing
this?

_____

_____

_____

_____

Blameless (3:13). Paul speaks quite often about the
need for being "blameless." The term refers not to
absolute, sinless perfection, but to wholehearted,
unmixed devotion to doing God's will in all things.
The concept is rooted in the Old Testament (Genesis 6:8-9; 17:1; Deuteronomy 18:13; Job 1:1,8; 2:3;
8:20; Psalm 15:1-2; 101:2; 119:1,80; Proverbs 2:7;
11:5; 19:1; 20:7; 28:18). Paul uses the term in
1 Corinthians 1:8; Ephesians 1:4, 5:27; Philippians
1:10, 2:15, and many other places.

Your response

12. a. What truth from 3:6-13 would you like to take to
heart this week?

_____

_____

_____

_____

For Further Study:
Add to your outline of
1 Thessalonians by
outlining 3:6-13.

Optional Application:
Based on Paul's prayer
in 1 Thessalonians
3:11-13, construct a
prayer you can use for
yourself or for others.
Memorize the prayer
and start putting it
into action.

b. What would you like to do about it?

_____

_____

_____

_____

13. List any questions you have about 3:6-13.

_____

_____

_____

_____

For the group

By now you can see that spiritual parenting is a theme
of this letter. When he was with the Thessalonians,
Paul acted as mother and father to them (2:7-12). Their
stability gives him the kind of intense joy that a child's
success gives most parents. What do you make of the
bond between Paul and his spiritual offspring? Does
anyone in your group have a spiritual parent like this?
Does anyone have spiritual children? Do you want to
have spiritual children? These are just a few of the
questions you could use to start your discussion
around this topic.

1 Thessalonians 4:1-12

Living to Please God

Chapters 1–3 of 1 Thessalonians contain personal messages of commendation for the Thessalonian believers as well as explanations of the missionaries' activities and motives. In chapters 4–5, Paul focuses on giving practical instruction to the Thessalonians in matters relating to "what is lacking in your faith" (3:10).

As always, read 4:1-12 several times. Read it aloud at least once. Get a feel for what Paul's concerns are for the Thessalonians.

1. This passage breaks down nicely into three sections, each relating in some way to proper Christian living. Summarize Paul's main point in each of the following:

   4:1-2 _____

   _____

   _____

   4:3-8 _____

   _____

   _____

   4:9-12 _____

   _____

   _____

57

Pleasing God should be a top priority for all Christians. Central passages on this important topic include Romans 14:17-18, 2 Corinthians 5:9-10, Ephesians 5:8-10, and Colossians 1:9-14.

For Thought and Discussion: Why do you think Paul felt the need to remind the Thessalonians that his instructions to them were given under the authority of Jesus Christ (4:1-2)?

2. Scan 4:1-2,6,11. Notice how often Paul comes back to various points that he has already told them. What were some of the things Paul felt were important enough to tell the Thessalonians before he left them?

_____

_____

_____

_____

_____

_____

_____

3. Read 4:1,10. What do the phrases "do this more and more" and "do so more and more" tell you about Paul's primary purpose in writing these words of instruction to the Thessalonians?

_____

_____

_____

_____

Instructions (4:2). This word was often used by the Greeks in a military context for the commands given by an officer to his men. It is thus a word with a ring of authority (Acts 5:28, 16:24).

The Christian and sexual immorality

Sanctified (4:3). Literally "set apart" as holy to God. Christians have been "bought with a price" (1 Corinthians 6:20), and are now to be "set apart" for His service. Flirtations with the world system are not an option for the Christian.

Sexual immorality (4:3). In its narrow sense, the word *porneia* originally referred to sexual acts connected with the worship of sexuality in pagan rites—sex with a temple prostitute. Jews (of whom Paul was one) used the word for all the sexual activities practiced by Gentiles that were forbidden in Jewish law, including premarital and extramarital intercourse, adultery, homosexuality, and bestiality. We might add to the list pornography and any activities of sexual addiction, which reflect a kind of idolatry.

4. a. What is God's will regarding the Christian's use of his body (4:4)?

_____

_____

_____

b. This is an important issue. In order to gain a fuller understanding of Paul's teachings on how the Christian is to use his body, examine and summarize each of the following passages in a short sentence:

Romans 6:19 _____

_____

_____

_____

Romans 12:1 _____

_____

_____

_____

1 Corinthians 6:13-20 (especially 6:20) _____

_____

_____

_____

59

Philippians 1:20-24 _____

_____

_____

_____

_____

_____

c. What insights do these passages give you in
regard to your understanding of 1 Thessalonians
4:3-6?

_____

_____

_____

_____

_____

5. Read 4:5, and notice how it contrasts with 4:4.

a. Paul describes "the heathen" as those "who do
not know God." What does "knowing God"
involve according to the following passages?

Jeremiah 9:23-24 _____

_____

_____

_____

_____

1 John 2:4-6, 4:7-8 _____

_____

_____

_____

_____

b. Is it possible for someone to "know God" as these passages indicate and at the same time engage in sexual immorality? Explain.

_____

_____

_____

_____

6. Read 4:6. In what ways is it possible to "wrong" a brother in regard to the issue of sexual immorality?

_____

_____

_____

_____

_____

Live a holy life (4:7). Literally, "Live within the sphere of sanctification." This phrase conveys the thought of atmosphere. The atmosphere for the believer is sanctification (i.e., being "set apart" as holy for God's service and use). Sanctification is the very air the Christian breathes.

Rejects (4:8). Carries the meaning "to hold as null and void," or "to treat with utter indifference."

7. There are three different references to God in 4:6-8. These verses indicate that each Person in the Trinity is involved in the lives of the Thessalonians. Keeping in mind that *God* is normally used to refer to the Father while *Lord* normally is used for Jesus Christ, summarize how each Person of the Trinity relates to Paul's command about holy living.

Jesus Christ (4:6) _____

_____

_____

For Further Study: For more on God as the Avenger of evil deeds, take a look at Deuteronomy 32:35; Romans 2:5-11, 12:19; and Hebrews 10:30-31. How does this relate to the idea that God is love (1 John 4:8)? Is it a contradiction? Explain.

For Thought and Discussion: What images does living a holy life bring to your mind? Do you think of a nun who never smiles? Of a person with no passion and no fun? Someone you know?

Optional Application: Sexual immorality seems to be a universal problem. In view of this:
    a. Do you need to make any decisions regarding the movies, video tapes, magazines, television shows, etc., that are part of your life?
    b. Do you need to deal with any improper relationships in view of what God's will is for your life (1 Thessalonians 4:3)?
    c. Are there any activities you need to curtail that are prompting lust in your life?

61

The Father (4:7) _____

_____

_____

_____

_____

The Holy Spirit (4:8) _____

_____

_____

_____

_____

Brotherly love

Brotherly love (4:9). This is a translation of the Greek word *philadelphia*, a word that—in nonreligious contexts—was used to refer to the mutual love of the children of the same father. In the first century, believing in Christ often resulted in the rupturing of family ties. But as Christians, they became part of a new family (the heavenly Father's); hence, they became brothers of all who believed.

Macedonia (4:10). Paul's team had left pockets of believers in towns across Macedonia: in Philippi, Berea, and Thessalonica. The believers were tiny minorities in all three towns, all facing the disgust or rage of their neighbors. Although miles apart without transportation faster than walking, the three fledgling churches were evidently in touch with each other.

8. What do you think Paul means when he says that the Thessalonians have been "taught by God" to love each other (4:9)?

_____

_____

_____

_____

For Further Study:
For more practical truths on love, take a look at Romans 12:9-16, 1 Corinthians 13:1-7, Hebrews 13:1-3, 1 Peter 1:22, and 1 John 3:16-18. It might be helpful for you to try to refine what these passages teach about love by summarizing all your findings into a single paragraph.

9. A present tense verb in the Greek language indicates a continuous, perpetual activity. This is the form of the word *love* in 4:10. How would it be possible continually, perpetually, and actively to love all the brothers and sisters in Macedonia? What might that look like in practice?

_____

_____

_____

_____

_____

Quiet (4:11). Literally, "undisturbed, settled, restful."

10. Nowhere in 1 Thessalonians does Paul exhort his readers to evangelize the neighborhood in the sense of preaching. (The same is true in his other letters.) Instead, he outlines a very different evangelism strategy in 4:11-12. What is that strategy?

_____

_____

_____

_____

_____

For Thought and Discussion: Paul had a high opinion of ordinary work, which in his day meant manual labor (4:11). As we know, he set an example by supporting himself through making tents. Are you surprised that Paul had such respect for "secular," even "blue collar" work? Explain.

For Further Study: Cross references to consider on how we act toward "outsiders" (nonChristians) include Colossians 4:5-6 and 1 Timothy 3:7.

For Further Study: Continue your outline of 1 Thessalonians by outlining 4:1-12.

11. Why would doing these things in spite of hostility from others draw favorable attention from outsiders?

_____

_____

_____

_____

_____

_____

12. Why do you suppose Paul didn't tell the Thessalonian believers to "witness" to their neighbors?

_____

_____

_____

_____

13. A good way to ensure that you understand the meaning of a passage is to paraphrase it in your own words. Take a few moments to paraphrase 4:1-12. Include not only the content of the passage but try to get behind the words to the feelings and emotions that permeate this passage.

_____

_____

_____

_____

_____

_____

Your response

Have you ever considered what impact your capacity to love has on other people? In the second century AD,

Tertullian said: "Behold how these Christians love each other."[1] He was talking about practical love, such as taking care of prisoners, the sick, and the poor. Lucian, who was an unbelieving Greek writer of the same century, said: "It is incredible to see the fervour with which the people of that religion help each other in their wants. They spare nothing. Their first legislator [Jesus] has put it into their heads that they are all brethren."[2]

14. What can you do this week to love "more and more" (4:10)?

_____

_____

_____

_____

15. List any questions you have about this passage.

_____

_____

_____

_____

For the group

Discuss what steps you can take "so that your daily life may win the respect of outsiders" (4:12). Be creative. You might raise the issue of how each person in the group was at one time an "outsider." Ask the question: Did anyone in the group initially become interested in Christianity as a result of coming to respect the behavior and lifestyle of a Christian with whom he or she came into contact? Following this, you can focus the discussion on specific steps that can be taken to imitate such behavior in daily living.

Paganism and Sexual Immorality
The Thessalonians lived in a society where sexual promiscuity was openly permitted and encouraged
(continued on page 66)

65

(continued from page 65)

for men. Greek religion often included sacred prostitution as a form of worship to gods and goddesses who embodied the forces of nature. Many pagan temples housed priestesses whose task was to have intercourse with male worshipers and thereby give them contact with the divine. The keeping of mistresses and/or young male lovers was a common practice among the upper classes, while common men frequented the temples. Sex was regarded as a man's need, as indifferent as food and drink. In view of this, it is understandable that Christians recently converted, like the Thessalonians, were assaulted on a daily basis by sexual temptations. To be faithful to one's wife was almost unheard-of. (Women who were not prostitutes were considered property of their husbands, and their infidelities could be punished, although drunken revelry during festivals did relax the rules.)

1. Cited by Leon Morris, *The First and Second Epistles to the Thessalonians* (Grand Rapids, MI: Eerdmans, 1979), page 129.
2. Cited by Irving L. Jensen, *1 & 2 Thessalonians* (Chicago: Moody, 1987), page 52.

1 Thessalonians 4:13-18

Comfort for Bereaved Christians

Timothy returned from visiting Thessalonica with a list of questions about which the believers there were concerned. Apparently, one of these concerns had to do with Christians who died before Christ returned. Before His death, Jesus had promised to come back to earth at some point to take His followers with Him to His Father (John 14:3). Paul had probably told the Thessalonians of this promise. Jesus had deliberately refused to give any indication of when He was coming back (John 21:22, Acts 1:7), but for many years His disciples assumed He would come within their lifetimes. The Thessalonians evidently assumed this. They may also have assumed that Christ's promise of "eternal life" meant none of them would die before the Lord's return. But to their shock and dismay, some of them did die shortly after Paul left them. Whether they died of natural causes or as a result of persecution we don't know, but the deaths disturbed the Thessalonians enough that they asked Timothy to get an explanation from Paul. Would these departed believers miss out on the grand event when Christ returned for His people? Would death rob them of participating?

Begin your time of study by reading 4:13-18 several times. Read it aloud at least once.

1. What initial questions do you have about this passage before you begin the study?

_____

_____

_____

_____

_____

_____

Asleep (4:13). Sleep is a common figure of speech for death in the New Testament (e.g., John 11:11).

Who have no hope (4:13). Inscriptions on ancient tombs reveal that people of the first century viewed death with horror and dread. Some religions and philosophies taught that the soul was immortal and longed to be freed from the body at death, but most said souls of the dead lived in a shadowy underworld. No one looked forward to that underworld state, and religions that promised ways to escape it were becoming increasingly popular in Paul's time.

2. Verse 13 sets the theme for the entire passage. Paraphrase this verse in your own words.

_____

_____

_____

_____

_____

3. Jesus wept when His friend Lazarus died, even though He was about to restore Lazarus' life (John 11:32-36). Still, how does a Christian's grief at a loved one's death differ from the grief others might suffer?

_____

_____

_____

_____

4. Paul indicates that when a Christian dies, his body "sleeps" until Christ returns to earth. This raises the question: Where does the Christian's spirit go when this happens? Read 2 Corinthians 5:8 and Philippians 1:23-24, and summarize your findings.

_____

_____

_____

_____

_____

For Further Study: For more on the importance of Christ's resurrection, take a look at 1 Corinthians 15 (especially verses 14, 17-22). Cross references include Acts 17:31; Romans 1:1-4, 4:25; 2 Corinthians 4:14; Ephesians 1:19-22; and Hebrews 4:14-16.

5. What is Paul's basis of assurance that departed believers are now with the Lord and will come back with Him when He returns (1 Thessalonians 4:14)?

_____

_____

_____

_____

According to the Lord's own word (4:15). Scholars are not sure what Paul means by this. Possible interpretations of the phrase are: (1) Sayings of Jesus not recorded in the four New Testament Gospels. That there are such sayings is clear from Acts 20:35, where Jesus is quoted as saying something found in none of the Gospel accounts. (2) Or, Paul may have received a special revelation directly from the Lord (compare 2 Corinthians 12:1 and Galatians 1:12).

6. Why do you think Paul emphasized to the Thessalonians that his teachings on this subject were based on "the Lord's own word" (4:15)?

_____

_____

_____

For Further Study:
The word translated as "caught up" is also used in Acts 8:39 and 2 Corinthians 12:2,4. What insights do these verses give you into 1 Thessalonians 4:17?

_____

_____

7. What does Paul mean when he says that those Christians who are alive when Christ comes will not "precede" those who have died (4:15-18)?

_____

_____

_____

_____

_____

With the voice of the archangel (4:16). There are two possible meanings: (1) This may refer to Jesus speaking with "an archangel-type voice" (i.e., a voice of majesty, power, and authority); or (2) an archangel may be present with Jesus and take part in the event. Michael is the only archangel named in Scripture (Jude 9).

Trumpet call (4:16). Trumpets are often used in Scripture as signs of assembling, of warning, or of taking a new step (Isaiah 27:13, Joel 2:1, and Zechariah 9:14). The ancients used trumpets to call armies to assembly and to order a forward march.

Dead in Christ (4:16). Those who have trusted in Christ for salvation and have since died.

Clouds (4:17). Clouds are often mentioned in connection with the Second Coming of Christ (Matthew 24:30, Revelation 1:7; compare Acts 1:9).

Caught up (4:17). Literally, "seized up suddenly." The Latin for this word is *rapio*, from which we get the English word *rapture*. This event, when Christ catches up His people to be with Him, is often called the Rapture.

8. What three sounds will initiate the Rapture, and what do you think is the significance of each (4:16)?

sounds	significance

9. What is the first thing that happens after these sounds (4:16)?

_____

_____

10. What is the second thing that happens after these sounds (4:17)?

_____

_____

Bodily Resurrection

At the Rapture, Christians (both living and departed) will receive body upgrades. Many educated Greeks of Paul's day believed in an immortal soul, but they believed that the human body was inferior to the soul, a prison to be endured during this life. Paul's teaching of bodily resurrection consequently drew sneers from the intellectual elite of his day (Acts 17:32).

Educated believers in Corinth (a Greek city) had a tremendously hard time swallowing the notion of bodily resurrection. After all, everybody knew that a body decays within a short time after death and becomes part of the earth. How could Christ reassemble a body after its atoms (the Greeks had a rudimentary notion of atoms) had scattered and become building blocks for dirt and plants and even animals? Furthermore, at what age and physical condition would a resurrected person be? At the age of his death? At age fifteen or twenty? Anyone who thought about it long enough could come up with all kinds of reasons why bodily resurrection was farfetched. Paul took on objections like these in 1 Corinthians 15.

For Further Study:
For more on what a
spiritual body might be
like, consider Jesus'
body after His
resurrection. He could
walk through locked
doors but also be
touched and eat fish
(Luke 24:36-43, John
20:19-28).

Optional Application:
Do Paul's words offer
you any comfort in the
death of someone you
love?

11. a. What do you learn about the nature of a resurrected body from 1 Corinthians 15:35-55?

_____

_____

_____

_____

_____

_____

b. What do you think a "spiritual body" (1 Corinthians 15:44) is like? How would it differ from, say,
a disembodied spirit or a body like those we have
now?

_____

_____

_____

_____

_____

12. Paul did not write about the Rapture in order to
give a prophetic time line. What was his purpose
according to 1 Thessalonians 4:18?

_____

_____

_____

13. What can you deduce about the Thessalonians'
probable emotional state from 4:18?

_____

_____

14. Actually, 4:16-17 offer three different sources of
encouragement for the Thessalonians. How would
each of these comfort a suffering group of believers:

72

Resurrection of dead believers _____

_____

_____

_____

Translation of living believers _____

_____

_____

_____

Reunion of dead and living believers_____

_____

_____

_____

15. A good way to ensure that you understand a passage of Scripture is to summarize it in your own words. Take a few moments to summarize 4:13-18.

_____

_____

_____

_____

Your response

16. What difference does this guarantee of the Lord's return for His people, living and dead, make to you in your day-to-day life?

_____

_____

_____

_____

For Further Study:
Continue your outline of 1 Thessalonians by outlining 4:13-18.

Optional Application:
Meditate a few moments on the last part of 4:17: "And so we will be with the Lord forever." Make an effort in the coming week to start developing a more eternal perspective. Temporal problems often seem to dim in the light of such a perspective.

17. List any questions you still have about this passage.

_____

_____

_____

_____

_____

_____

For the group

One of the more sobering phrases found in the Bible is 1 Thessalonians 4:13: "the rest of men, who have no hope." Discuss the various ways that modern people attempt to deal with their own mortality. You might want to address the following questions in your discussion: What symptoms of this lack of hope do you see in modern society? What false cures can you think of that people have used in attempting to deal with this lack of hope apart from God?

1 Thessalonians 5:1-11

An Attitude of Watchfulness

The previous section of Paul's letter presented the joyful hope of the Rapture. The present passage contains a solemn warning that is the other side of that hope. These paragraphs discuss "the day of the Lord," a prophesied event that is much discussed in both the Old and New Testaments. Many such references indicate that much of what happens on this "day" is destructive.

In the present passage, Paul discusses how this day will come, the impact it will have on nonChristians, and how it relates to Christians.

Begin your study by reading through 5:1-11 several times. As you go through this passage, pay special attention to connecting words. Words like "therefore," "for," "but," etc., are indicators of how different verses relate to each other.

Times and dates

Day of the Lord (5:2). "The day of the Lord is a future period of time in which God will be at work in world affairs more directly and dramatically than He has been since the earthly ministry of the Lord Jesus Christ."[1] This extended "day" includes the Second Coming of the Lord and the Rapture, as well as judgment for those who reject Christ.

Jesus
Himself used the "thief
in the night" figure in
Matthew 24:42-44. How
does He say we should
live in light of our
ignorance about when
He will come?

For Further Study:
"The day of the Lord" is
a massive concept in
the Bible. Cross-
references for this
concept include Isaiah
2:12, 13:6,9; Ezekiel
13:5, 30:3; Joel 1:15;
Amos 5:18; Zephaniah
1:7,14; Acts 2:20;
2 Thessalonians 2:2;
and 2 Peter 3:10. Go
through these passages,
paying particular
attention to the
characteristics of
this "day."

1. What does 5:1-2 indicate about how thorough Paul
had been in his original instructions about "the day
of the Lord" to the Thessalonians?

_____

_____

2. Even though Paul had already told the Thessalonians that Jesus would come at an unexpected time,
like "a thief in the night," they still evidently
wanted to know when it would happen. Why do
you suppose people desire so strongly to forecast a
date for Christ's return?

_____

_____

_____

3. What does Jesus say in Matthew 24:36 about fore-
casting dates for His return?

_____

_____

_____

Peace and safety (5:3). The word *peace* indicates a
complete absence of alarm. "Safety" is used in the
sense of blind security. Under the circumstances,
these two words indicate a total misapprehension
of the very real danger that is present.

Destruction (5:3). This refers not to annihilation, but
to the breaking up of their peace and security by
God's direct intervention via judgment.

4. Why do you think the pronouns change from
"you" and "we" in 1 Thessalonians 5:1-2 to "they"
and "them" in 5:3? Who do "they" and "them"
refer to?

_____

_____

76

_____

_____

5. What is going to happen to them?

_____

_____

_____

6. Why do you think they are saying "peace and safety" (5:3) when danger is so near?

_____

_____

_____

_____

7. Paul compares the coming of destruction to the coming of labor pains. What does that image evoke for you? What does it say about the destruction?

_____

_____

_____

_____

For Thought and Discussion: What does it mean, in practical terms, to be "in darkness" (5:4)? How does living in spiritual darkness affect a person day to day?

For Further Study: The figure of a woman in labor comes up often in Scripture. See Isaiah 13:8, Jeremiah 4:31, Hosea 13:13, Matthew 24:8, Mark 13:8, and Galatians 4:19. Pay close attention to the particular meaning the figure is intended to convey in its context.

Sons of the Light

In 5:4, Paul switches the pronouns back to "you" to draw a contrast with "them."

8. As Paul says in Colossians 1:13-14, why are the Thessalonians not in darkness?

_____

_____

_____

_____

Optional Application:
What will being alert and self-controlled look like in your life this week? Can you think of some practical ways in which you need to be alert?

For Further Study:
On how Christians should live as children of light, see Ephesians 5:8-20.

For Further Study:
Look at 1 Corinthians 1:7; Titus 2:12; Hebrews 9:28; 1 Peter 1:13, 4:7; and 2 Peter 3:11-12. Based on these passages, summarize what kind of lifestyle God wants us to have as we await the Lord's coming.

Sons of the light (5:5). In Semitic thought, to be a "son" of something means to be characterized by that particular thing. Hence, "sons of the light" means "people characterized by light."

Asleep (5:6). This is a different word than that used three times in 4:13-15 (where "sleep" carries the meaning of "death"). The word in the present passage means "spiritual lethargy and insensitivity." This is the condition of all the unsaved.

9. According to 1 Thessalonians 5:4-8, how does a person who belongs to the light think and behave?

_____

_____

_____

_____

_____

10. Even though we don't know when the day of the Lord will come, why won't it overtake Christians as a surprise?

_____

_____

_____

11. a. The breastplate and the helmet were probably the most important items in a soldier's suit of armor because they protected the most important organs. What does this imagery tell you about the importance of faith, love, and hope in Paul's thinking (5:8)?

_____

_____

_____

_____

b. In what ways are faith, love, and hope protective gear in these times of suffering before the Lord comes? Give an example of how one of them protects us.

_____

_____

_____

_____

_____

Optional Application: Does your hope of eventual deliverance help protect you from buckling under the stresses of life? Or does salvation feel a long way off?

For Thought and Discussion: Paul often likened the Christian to a soldier with armor (Romans 13:12; 2 Corinthians 6:7, 10:4; Ephesians 6:10-18). Why do you think he used this military image so much? Do you find it helpful in understanding the spiritual life? Explain.

12. How do you think Paul intended the Thessalonians to go about "putting on" faith, love, and hope as armor? What does this mean in practical terms?

_____

_____

_____

_____

_____

13. How do you think the Thessalonians felt when reminded that the children of darkness who were persecuting them were destined for "wrath" (5:9)?

_____

_____

_____

_____

14. How do you feel when you think of unbelievers you know suffering wrath when the Lord comes? (Are you glad that they will receive justice? Are you nervous? Does the idea seem unreal?)

_____

_____

_____

Optional Application:
Do you know anyone
who might be
encouraged by what
Paul says in 5:1-11?
What can you say to
that person?

_____

_____

_____

He died (5:10). Note that Paul did not say that Christ
was killed. Jesus laid down His own life; no one
took it from Him (John 10:18). Furthermore, He
died "for us."

Whether we are awake or asleep (5:10). Scholars
interpret this in two ways: (1) "Whether we are
alive or dead"; or (2) "Whether we are spiritually
alert or lethargic." Many argue that the second
view is preferred in view of the fact that the word
for "asleep" is the same as that used in 5:6 (where
it clearly refers to spiritual lethargy).

15. Meditate on 5:9-10 for a few moments. How does
Paul foster the "hope of salvation" here (5:8)?

_____

_____

_____

_____

_____

16. The verbs "encourage" and "build up" (5:11) are in
a tense that indicate a continuous, habitual action.
These are to be done perpetually. Why would Paul
consider continual encouragement and upbuilding
so important to the spiritual growth and survival of
the Thessalonians?

_____

_____

_____

_____

_____

80

Your response

17. a. What do you want to take to heart from 5:1-11?

_____

_____

_____

_____

b. What do you want to do about it?

_____

_____

_____

_____

18. List any questions you have about this passage.

_____

_____

_____

_____

_____

For Further Study:
It's time to extend your outline of 1 Thes-salonians. Even if you have not been working on an outline, try outlining 5:1-11.

Optional Application:
Have a personal time of praise and thanksgiving to God for what He has done for you according to 5:9-10.

For the group

What practical steps can we take to "put on" faith and love as a breastplate and the hope of salvation as a helmet? Be creative. Consider your group as a Think Tank with the assigned task of coming up with usable, applicable guidelines for "putting on" faith, love, and hope. You might consider having each member of your group come up with his or her own list of guidelines during the next week or so. You can share your results with each other at the beginning of the next meeting.

1. Thomas L. Constable, "1 Thessalonians," in *The Bible Knowl-edge Commentary* (Grand Rapids, MI: Victor Books, 1983), page 705.

1 Thessalonians 5:12-15

Life in the Church

All of the members of the Thessalonian church were new converts; the church had only been in existence for a few months. As in other cities, Paul identified a few of the members as being best capable of leading the group. None of these, however, had any formal training other than what Paul was able to communicate to them in the short time he was with them.

It is understandable that some of the other new believers raised questions like, "Who is he to take the place of leadership in the church?" The Thessalonians were fully aware that their "leaders" were essentially as new to the faith as they were. The subsequent temptation was to pay them little or no respect. Timothy no doubt brought this problem to Paul's attention after his follow-up visit to Thessalonica.

In response, Paul felt it wise to say a few words in this letter to clear the matter up. He recognized that a church with little respect for its leadership was headed for failure. He accordingly addressed this issue with hopes of resolving it before it became too big to handle easily.

Read 5:12-15 several times, at least once aloud.

1. Make a list of issues Paul addresses in this short section.

   _____

   _____

   _____

In view of what you have
learned about proper
relationships with church
leaders (5:12-13), is
there any area of your
own behavior about
which you feel convicted
and in need of change?
If so, what do you need
to do?

Respect church elders

Those (5:12). Probably refers to elders of the church
appointed by Paul, as in Acts 14:23. That Paul uses
the plural ("those") indicates that there was more
than one elder in the Thessalonian church, as was
true in other churches to whom Paul wrote (see
Philippians 1:1).

Work hard (5:12). The elders probably carried full-time
jobs outside the church. This means that any work
they did in a church context would have been in
their spare time.

Live in peace (5:13). This is not a mere exhortation,
but an authoritative command from Paul. It is not
something open to negotiation. Paul orders them
to live in peace.

2. What two admonitions does Paul give the Thessalonians in regard to their church leaders in 5:12-13?

3. What is the significance of Paul's referring to the
church leaders as those who are "over you in the
Lord"?

4. Why should the Thessalonians hold their leaders in high regard (5:13)? What "work" is Paul talking about?

_____

_____

_____

_____

_____

5. Why do you think Paul deemed it necessary to tell all the Thessalonians, both leaders and led, to live at peace with each other (5:13)?

_____

_____

_____

_____

_____

For Further Study: For a discussion on the qualifications of elders, take a look at 1 Timothy 3:1-7 and Titus 1:6-9. Take a few minutes and make a list of such qualifications. These would be the characteristics Paul looked for in choosing elders at the church in Thessalonica.

For Thought and Discussion: Does holding leaders in highest regard mean never voicing your disagreements? Explain.

Relationships in the church

Idle (5:14). This military word originally referred to a soldier who was out of step or to an army moving about in disarray. The word eventually came to mean "that which is out of order" in a more general sense. "It is not idleness in the sense of legitimate leisure that is meant, but loafing. The use of this word makes it quite clear that there were some at Thessalonica who had ceased to work and were imposing on the generosity of others."[1]

Patient (5:14). Literally, "strong-tempered." It carries the idea of being tough and durable with a quiet and steady strength, even in the midst of intense pressure and hardship.

6. What four admonitions did Paul give the Thessalonians in 5:14? Put them in your own words, explaining what you think he meant.

admonitions	meaning

7. a. Skip ahead to Paul's second letter to the Thessalonians (written about a year after 1 Thessalonians). Read 2 Thessalonians 3:6-15. What insights does this passage give you regarding Paul's instructions to "warn those who are idle" in 1 Thessalonians 5:14? What was the situation a year after Paul gave that initial warning?

_____

_____

_____

_____

_____

b. Why do you suppose some able-bodied members of the church felt they didn't have to work and could let others support them?

_____

_____

_____

_____

8. On the other hand, Paul said it was legitimate—even important—to "help the weak." What's the difference between the weak and the idle?

_____

_____

_____

_____

9. Paul told the Thessalonians to "be patient with everyone" (5:14). He spoke of patience in many of his letters. Patience is an essential quality of love (1 Corinthians 13:4) and a result of the Holy Spirit's activity in our lives (Galatians 5:22). Why would patience be especially necessary for a young church with inexperienced church leaders on the one hand and imbalanced behavior among church members on the other hand?

_____

_____

_____

_____

_____

_____

Be kind (5:15). The tense of this verb indicates that kindness was to be a continuous, habitual activity. Paul reinforced this with the adverb "always."

10. How is "paying back wrong for wrong" (5:15) a direct contrast to patience?

_____

_____

_____

_____

For Thought and Discussion: In Romans 14:1-5 and 15:1-2, Paul talks about helping the spiritually weak. He says those whose faith is weak require more rules and structure to keep them growing in Christ than do those whose faith is stronger. What do you make of that? Do you think of weak faith as the reason why people need rules about eating and drinking and keeping special days?

Optional Application: What are some ways that you could apply what you have learned about patience at home? At your workplace? At church? With yourself?

For Thought and Discussion: What does it mean in practice to be kind to those who do wrong to us? Should we just pretend it never happened?

Optional Application: Meditate for a few moments on relationships you have with nonbelievers. What implications does Paul's exhortation to be kind "to everyone else" (5:15) have for your personal relationships with nonbelievers?

11. Why is it so essential for us to learn not to pay back wrong for wrong?

_____
_____
_____
_____
_____

12. a. Paul even urged kindness not only to fellow believers ("each other") but also "to everyone else." Why would this have been a challenge for the Thessalonians?

_____
_____
_____
_____
_____

b. Why was it nonetheless important?

_____
_____
_____
_____
_____

Your response

13. a. What seems most relevant to you in this paragraph of 1 Thessalonians?

_____
_____
_____

_____

_____

_____

For Further Study:
Continue your outline of
1 Thessalonians by
outlining 5:12-15.

b. Is there a step you can take to act on this? What is it?

_____

_____

_____

_____

14. List any questions you have about 1 Thessalonians 5:12-15.

_____

_____

_____

_____

For the group

Paul indicates in this passage that Christians have a mutual responsibility toward each other. Discuss the implications this has for your own group situation as well as for your personal relationships with each other. You might include in your discussion how all of this relates to the idea that each Christian is a part of the "body of Christ," and that each part of the body needs every other part (compare with 1 Corinthians 12:12-31).

1. Leon Morris, *The First and Second Epistles to the Thessalonians* (Grand Rapids, MI: Eerdmans, 1979), page 168.

1 Thessalonians 5:16-24

Holy Living

Begin your own time of study by reading 5:16-24 several times. Read it aloud at least once.

1. Summarize the three sections of this passage using a short sentence for each:

   5:16-18 _____

   _____

   _____

   _____

   5:19-22 _____

   _____

   _____

   _____

   5:23-24 _____

   _____

   _____

   _____

For Further Study:
For Further Study:
For more on Christian
joy, look at Matthew
5:12; Acts 15:31;
Romans 5:2;
 2 Corinthians 8:1-2;
Philippians 3:1 and 4:4.
What do these passages
indicate about the
foundation of Christian
joy?

2. This passage contains some final instructions from Paul to the Thessalonians. What do you think Paul is trying to accomplish here?

_____

_____

_____

_____

Joy, prayer, and thanks

3. How do you think 5:16-18 connects to the previous paragraph?

_____

_____

_____

_____

4. a. Paul was not just presenting "dry theory" to the Thessalonians when he told them to "be joyful always." Read Acts 16:22-25. This episode occurred less than a year before Paul wrote 1 Thessalonians. What was Paul's experience of being joyful always?

_____

_____

_____

_____

b. How easy is it for you to be joyful while suffering that badly? Why do you think that is?

_____

_____

_____

_____

Continually (5:17). This word was used in the Greek world to refer to the lingering persistency of a hacking cough. "Just as a person with a hacking cough is not always audibly coughing though the tendency to cough is always there, so the Christian who prays without ceasing is not always praying audibly and yet prayer is always the attitude of his heart and life."[1]

For Thought and Discussion: How does a person pray continually? Describe what you think that involves.

5. What's the connection between joy (5:16) and prayer (5:17)?

_____

_____

_____

_____

Optional Application: Take a day to concentrate on continual prayer as much as possible. Your prayer can be as simple as calling to mind grateful thoughts of God.

Optional Application: With a thorough concordance, do a word study on "rejoicing." Look up some of the main references to "rejoicing" and "joy," paying particular attention to the source of such joy. Based on your study, formulate a few easy-to-remember principles for joyful living. Then memorize them and put them to work.

Christ Jesus (5:18). This is a compound name that emphasizes both the deity and humanity of our Lord.

6. a. Paul urges the Thessalonians to "give thanks in all circumstances" (5:18). What is the significance of Paul using the word "in" as opposed to "for"?

_____

_____

_____

_____

Optional Application: Are you joyful? Why do you think you are that way?

b. As a cross reference, read Romans 8:28. What insights does this passage give you in your understanding of Paul's admonition in 1 Thessalonians 5:18?

_____

_____

_____

_____

_____

_____

Final instructions

7. Read 5:19-22. In this section Paul lists five commands in staccato fashion. Two of them are negative, three of them positive. List these, and make a note of any questions you have at this point as to what Paul's meaning may be.

commands (positive/negative)	your questions

8. Scripture often associates the Holy Spirit with fire (Matthew 3:11, Acts 2:3-4). What does this tell you about the Holy Spirit?

_____

_____

_____

_____

_____

_____

94

Do not put out the Spirit's fire (5:19). The phrase
  actually carries the idea "Stop putting out the
  Spirit's fire." Paul apparently wanted the Thessalonians to stop certain activities they were presently
  engaged in so the ministry of the Holy Spirit
  among them would be unhindered.

9. Based on the issues Paul has addressed in this letter, what might some of the activities be that the
   Thessalonians are to stop (5:19)?

   _____

   _____

   _____

   _____

   _____

   _____

   _____

   _____

**For Thought and
Discussion:** It's possible
that one of the ways the
Thessalonians were
putting out the Spirit's
fire (5:19) was by
making absolutely
nothing of certain
prophecies (5:20). Do
you think so? Explain.

**For Thought and
Discussion:** Do you
believe Paul's instruction
about testing prophecies
rather than treating
them with contempt has
any relevance today? If
so, how? If not, why not?

Prophecies (5:20). The gift of prophecy was the ability
  to receive and communicate direct revelations
  from God (1 Corinthians 13:8). These revelations
  sometimes concerned future events (Acts 11:28),
  but they often dealt with the present (Acts 13:2).

Contempt (5:20). Literally, "to make absolutely nothing of."

10. When Paul admonished the Thessalonians to "test
    everything" (5:21) in the context of speaking about
    "prophecies" (5:20), what do you think he had in
    mind? How would one test a prophecy? What
    insights do the following verses give you?

    Acts 17:11 _____

    _____

    _____

For Thought and Discussion: How is Paul's reference to God as "the God of peace" (5:23) significant in view of what Paul had just told the Thessalonians in 5:12-15?

For Thought and Discussion: In his reference to "spirit, soul and body" (5:23), do you think Paul is referring to three separate parts of humans, or is he using these words simply to denote the whole person? Why?

1 Corinthians 12:3_____

_____

_____

1 John 4:1-3_____

_____

_____

Every kind of evil (5:22). The primary root meaning of this word translated as "kind" is "that which meets the eye," or "the external appearance." Consequently, *The King James Version* translates this verse as "Avoid every appearance of evil." However, by Paul's day, the word had evolved to mean "kind," "sort," or "species." Modern translators believe Paul had this second meaning in mind and was not primarily concerned with keeping up appearances.

11. a. What do you think Paul is saying in 1 Thessalonians 5:22?

_____

_____

_____

_____

b. What connection do you see between avoiding evil and 5:19-21?

_____

_____

_____

_____

Paul's prayer

Kept (5:23). The root meaning of this word is "to watch over, to guard, to keep."

12. In his prayer recorded in 5:23, what request does Paul make in two different ways?

_____

_____

_____

_____

13. Why is it important to remember that God does the sanctifying and is responsible for making sure we are blameless when Christ comes?

_____

_____

_____

_____

14. a. What is the ground of Paul's trust (5:24)?

_____

_____

b. Why is it often hard for us to count on God's faithfulness?

_____

_____

_____

_____

Your response

15. a. What aspect of this passage would you like to take to heart this week?

_____

_____

_____

For Thought and Discussion: Paul has just finished instructing the Thessalonians on what they need to do to keep themselves holy (5:16-22). But in 5:23 he prays that *God* would sanctify them through and through. This touches on the issue of human responsibility versus divine sovereignty. Regarding the issue of holiness and sanctification, what precisely is man's role and what precisely is God's role?

For Further Study: Paul often refers to God as the "God of peace" in his letters. A few examples include Romans 15:33, 1 Corinthians 14:33, 2 Corinthians 13:11, and Philippians 4:9. Notice that such references always appear toward the end of each of his letters. Why do you think he does this?

For Further Study: Continue your outline of 1 Thessalonians by outlining 5:16-24. Let your three main divisions be 5:16-18, 5:19-22, and 5:23-24.

Optional Application:
Memorize the prayer in
5:23 and offer it up to
God in behalf of other
members in your group,
your friends, and your
family.

b. Is there anything concrete you can do about it?

_____

_____

_____

_____

16. List any questions you have about 5:16-24.

_____

_____

_____

_____

_____

For the group

Discuss Paul's admonition to "give thanks in all circumstances." In your discussion, you might address
difficult issues such as: How can we give thanks in circumstances involving terminal illness? Death? A mis-
carriage? Loss of a job? and so on. You can then close
your time together by offering thanks to God for His
work in your group and in each group member's life.

1. Charles C. Ryrie, *First and Second Thessalonians* (Chicago, IL:
Moody, 1968), page 80.

LESSON ELEVEN

1 Thessalonians 5:25-28 and Review

Looking Back

Closing words

Holy kiss (5:26). A kiss was a common greeting in the first century. A modern Western counterpart would be a handshake.

1. Why do you think Paul wanted this letter read to all the "brothers" (5:27)?

_____

_____

_____

_____

_____

2. Paul always ended his letters with a blessing of grace, as in 5:28. Why do you think he did this?

_____

_____

_____

_____

_____

For Further Study:
Using a thorough concordance, do a word study on "grace." Look up some of the major passages, and pay particular attention to the references that occur in Paul's writings. You might want to make a list of the various blessings God bestows on Christians on the basis of grace.

99

Review

3. Reread Paul's letter to the Thessalonians, and discuss here what you think were the most important lessons you learned from it about:

Faith _____

_____

_____

_____

_____

Love _____

_____

_____

_____

_____

Hope _____

_____

_____

_____

_____

Joy _____

_____

_____

_____

_____

Moral purity _____

_____

_____

_____

_____

Death _____

_____

_____

_____

_____

Other key lessons _____

_____

_____

_____

_____

_____

_____

_____

_____

_____

4. Scan through 1 Thessalonians once again. Are
   there any questions that seem important to you
   that remain unanswered? If so, some of the sources
   on pages 105-107 may help you to answer those
   questions. Or, you might want to study some particular passage with cross references of your own.

_____

_____

_____

_____

_____

If you have not already done so, you might want to try putting together your own outline of 1 Thessalonians. Such an outline—even an abbreviated one—will help you to retain much of what you have covered in your study. Experiment with the following procedure:

a. First, at the top of your paper, summarize what you think the book's main purpose is in a single sentence.

b. Let the two main divisions of your outline be 1–3 and 4–5.

c. Fill in as many supporting sections as you need in each division. Consult the chart on page 19 if you get stuck.

5. Have you noticed any areas (attitudes, opinions, thoughts, relationships with people, general behavior, etc.) in which you have changed as a result of studying Paul's first letter to the Thessalonian church? How have you changed?

_____

_____

_____

_____

_____

_____

6. Look back over the "Your response" sections in each lesson. Scan through those questions to which you expressed a desire to make some personal application. Are you satisfied with the way you have followed through? Take some time to pray about those areas you think you should continue to pursue. You might want to make note of any resolutions for the future here.

_____

_____

_____

_____

_____

_____

For the group

After going over the questions in this section, let anyone in the group pose any questions he or she still has about 1 Thessalonians. Allow others in the group to respond to such questions if they have any insights or answers. If the question remains unanswered, make plans for someone to check one of the sources on pages 105–107 for insights that might help. The results can be shared at the next meeting.

At this point, you may want to evaluate how well your group functioned during your study of 1 Thessalonians. Questions you might ask include:

- What did you learn about small-group study?
- How well did the members of the group behave like the body of Christ?
- Were the needs of individual members met on a regular basis? (If there was any failure in this, what changes can be made in the group to rectify the situation for future meetings?)
- Was everyone able to share ideas?
- Was your group prayer time fruitful?
- What steps can you take to meet the current needs of your group members?
- What will you do next?

STUDY AIDS

For further information on the material covered in this study, consider the following sources. If your local bookstore does not have them, ask the bookstore to order them from the publisher, or find them in a seminary library. Many university and public libraries also have these books.

Historical and Background Sources

Bruce, F. F. *New Testament History* (Doubleday, 1980).
> A readable history of Herodian kings, Roman governors, philosophical schools, Jewish sects, Jesus, the early Jerusalem church, Paul, and early Gentile Christianity. Well-documented with footnotes for the serious student, but the notes do not intrude.

Harrison, E. F. *Introduction to the New Testament* (Eerdmans, 1971).
> History from Alexander the Great—who made Greek culture dominant in the biblical world—through philosophies, pagan and Jewish religions, Jesus' ministry and teaching (the weakest section), and the spread of Christianity. Very good maps and photographs of the land, art, and architecture of New Testament times.

Packer, James I., Merril C. Tenney, William White, Jr. *The Bible Almanac* (Thomas Nelson, 1980).
> One of the most accessible handbooks of the people of the Bible and how they lived. Many photos and illustrations liven an already readable text.

Concordances, Dictionaries, and Handbooks

A *concordance* lists words of the Bible alphabetically along with each verse in which the word appears. It lets you do your own word studies. An *exhaustive* concordance lists every word used in a given translation, while an *abridged* or *complete* concordance omits either some words, some occurrences of the word, or both.

The two best exhaustive concordances are *Strong's Exhaustive Concordance* and *Young's Analytical Concordance to the Bible*. Both are available based on the

King James Version of the Bible and the New American Standard Bible. *Strong's* has an index by which you can find out which Greek or Hebrew word is used in a given English verse. *Young's* breaks up each English word it translates. However, neither concordance requires knowledge of the original language.

Among other good, less expensive concordances, *Cruden's Complete Concordance* is keyed to the King James and Revised Versions, and *The NIV Complete Concordance* is keyed to the New International Version. These include all references to every word included, but they omit "minor" words. They also lack indexes to the original languages.

A ***Bible dictionary*** or ***Bible encyclopedia*** alphabetically lists articles about people, places, doctrines, important words, customs, and geography of the Bible.

The New Bible Dictionary, edited by J. D. Douglas, F. F. Bruce, J. I. Packer, N. Hillyer, D. Guthrie, A.R. Millard, and D.J. Wiseman (Tyndale, 1982) is more comprehensive than most dictionaries. Its 1300 pages include quantities of information along with excellent maps, charts, diagrams, and an index for cross-referencing.

Unger's Bible Dictionary by Merrill F. Unger (Moody, 1979) is equally good and is available in an inexpensive paperback edition

The *Zondervan Pictorial Encyclopedia* edited by Merrill C. Tenney (Zondervan, 1975, 1976) is excellent and exhaustive, and is being revised and updated. However, its five 1000-page volumes are a financial investment, so all but very serious students may prefer to use it at a church, public, college, or seminary library.

Unlike a Bible dictionary in the above sense, *Vine's Expository Dictionary of New Testament Words* by W. E. Vine (various publishers) alphabetically lists major words used in the King James Version and defines each New Testament Greek word that KJV translates with that English word. *Vine's* lists verse references where that Greek word appears, so that you can do your own cross-references and word studies without knowing any Greek.

Vine's is a good basic book for beginners, but it is much less complete than other Greek helps for English speakers. More serious students might prefer *The New International Dictionary of New Testament Theology,* edited by Colin Brown (Zondervan), or *The Theological Dictionary of the New Testament* by Gerhard Kittel and Gerhard Friedrich, abridged in one volume by Geoffrey W. Bromiley (Eerdmans).

A ***Bible atlas*** can be a great aid to understanding what is going on in a book of the Bible and how geography affected events. Here is a list of a few good choices:

The Macmillan Atlas by Yohanan Aharoni and Michael Avi-Yonah (Macmillan, 1968, 1977) contains 264 maps, 89 photos, and 12 graphics. The many maps of individual events portray battles, movements of people, and changing boundaries in detail.

The New Bible Atlas by J. J. Bimson and J. P. Kane (Tyndale, 1985) has 73 maps, 34 photos, and 34 graphics. Its evangelical perspective, concise and helpful text, and excellent research make it a very useful purchase, but its greatest strength is its outstanding graphics, such as cross-sections of the Dead Sea.

The Bible Mapbook by Simon Jenkins (Lion, 1984) is much shorter and less expensive than most other atlases, so it offers a good first taste of the usefulness of maps. It contains 91 simple maps, very little text, and 20 graphics. Some of the graphics are computer-generated and intriguing.

The Moody Atlas of Bible Lands by Barry J. Beitzel (Moody, 1984) is scholarly, very evangelical, and full of theological text, indexes, and references. This admirable reference work will be too deep and costly for some, but Beitzel shows vividly how God prepared the land of Israel perfectly for the acts of salvation He was going to accomplish in it.

A **handbook** of biblical customs can also be useful. Some good ones are *Today's Handbook of Bible Times and Customs* by William L. Coleman (Bethany, 1984) and the less detailed *Daily Life in Bible Times* (Nelson, 1982).

For Small Group Leaders

The Small Group Leader's Handbook by Steve Barker et al. (InterVarsity, 1982).
Written by an InterVarsity small group with college students primarily in mind. It includes information on small group dynamics and how to lead in light of them, and many ideas for worship, building community, and outreach. It has a good chapter on doing inductive Bible study.

Getting Together: A Guide for Good Groups by Em Griffin (InterVarsity, 1982).
Applies to all kinds of groups, not just Bible studies. From his own experience, Griffin draws deep insights into why people join groups; how people relate to each other; and principles of leadership, decision making, and discussions. It is fun to read, but its 229 pages will take more time than the above book.

You Can Start a Bible Study Group by Gladys Hunt (Harold Shaw, 1984).
Builds on Hunt's thirty years of experience leading groups. This book is wonderfully focused on God's enabling. It is both clear and applicable for Bible study groups of all kinds.

How to Build a Small Groups Ministry by Neal F. McBride (NavPress, 1994).
This hands-on workbook for pastors and lay leaders includes everything you need to know to develop a plan that fits your unique church. Through basic principles, case studies, and worksheets, McBride leads you through twelve logical steps for organizing and administering a small groups ministry.

How to Lead Small Groups by Neal F. McBride (NavPress, 1990).
Covers leadership skills for all kinds of small groups—Bible study, fellowship, task, and support groups. Filled with step-by-step guidance and practical exercises to help you grasp the critical aspects of small group leadership and dynamics.

DJ Plus, a special section in *Discipleship Journal* (NavPress, bimonthly).
Unique. Three pages of this feature are packed with practical ideas for

small groups. Writers discuss what they are currently doing as small group members and leaders. To subscribe, write to Subscription Services, Post Office Box 54470, Boulder, Colorado 80323-4470.

Bible Study Methods

Braga, James. *How to Study the Bible* (Multnomah, 1982).
Clear chapters on a variety of approaches to Bible study: synthetic, geographical, cultural, historical, doctrinal, practical, and so on. Designed to help the ordinary person without seminary training to use these approaches.

Fee, Gordon, and Douglas Stuart. *How to Read the Bible For All Its Worth* (Zondervan, 1982).
After explaining in general what interpretation (exegesis) and application (hermeneutics) are, Fee and Stuart offer chapters on interpreting and applying the different kinds of writing in the Bible: Epistles, Gospels, Old Testament Law, Old Testament narrative, the Prophets, Psalms, Wisdom, and Revelation. Fee and Stuart also suggest good commentaries on each biblical book. They write as evangelical scholars who personally recognize Scripture as God's Word for their daily lives.

Jensen, Irving L. *Independent Bible Study* (Moody, 1963), and *Enjoy Your Bible* (Moody, 1962).
The former is a comprehensive introduction to the inductive Bible study method, especially the use of synthetic charts. The latter is a simpler introduction to the subject.

Wald, Oletta. *The Joy of Discovery in Bible Study* (Augsburg, 1975).
Wald focuses on issues such as how to observe all that is in a text, how to ask questions of a text, how to use grammar and passage structure to see the writer's point, and so on. Very helpful on these subjects.

Titles in the
Lifechange series:

BIBLE STUDIES AND SMALL-GROUP MATERIALS FROM NAVPRESS

BIBLE STUDY SERIES
Design for Discipleship
Foundation for Christian Living
God in You
Learning to Love
The Life and Ministry of
    Jesus Christ
LifeChange
Love One Another
Pilgrimage Guides
Radical Relationships
Studies in Christian Living
Thinking Through Discipleship

TOPICAL BIBLE STUDIES
Becoming a Woman of Excellence
Becoming a Woman of Freedom
Becoming a Woman of Prayer
Becoming a Woman of Purpose
The Blessing Study Guide
Celebrating Life!
Growing in Christ
Growing Strong in God's Family
Homemaking
Husbands and Wives
Intimacy with God
Jesus Cares for Women
Jesus Changes Women
Lessons on Assurance
Lessons on Christian Living
Loving Your Husband
Loving Your Wife
A Mother's Legacy
Parents and Children
Praying from God's Heart
Strategies for a Successful
    Marriage
Surviving Life in the Fast Lane
To Run and Not Grow Tired
To Stand and Not Be Moved
To Walk and Not Grow Weary

What God Does When Men Pray
When the Squeeze is On

BIBLE STUDIES WITH COMPANION BOOKS
Bold Love
Daughters of Eve
The Discipline of Grace
The Feminine Journey
From Bondage to Bonding
Hiding from Love
Inside Out
The Masculine Journey
The Practice of Godliness
The Pursuit of Holiness
Secret Longings of the Heart
Spiritual Disciplines for the
    Christian Life
Tame Your Fears
Transforming Grace
Trusting God
What Makes a Man?

SMALL-GROUP RESOURCES
201 Great Questions
Discipleship Journal's 101 Best
    Small-Group Ideas
How to Build a Small-Groups
    Ministry
How to Have Great Small-Group
    Meetings
How to Lead Small Groups
The Navigator Bible Studies
    Handbook
New Testament LessonMaker
The Small-Group Leaders
    Training Course

NAVPRESS
BRINGING TRUTH TO LIFE
www.navpress.org

Get your copies today at your local Christian bookstore, or call
(800) 366-7788 and ask for offer **NPBS**.

Turn your small group from just a bunch of people to a tightly knit community.

Does your small group feel like just a bunch of people? Do you long for greater intimacy and growth?

With Pilgrimage/NavPress Small-Group Training Seminars you can turn your small group into a community of believers excited to study God's Word and apply it to their lives. With new leadership skills and practical "how to" help, you'll be equipped to provide well-trained leadership and direction for your group, turning it from just a bunch of people to a community that supports and cares for one another.

Here's what you'll learn.
You'll learn ►how trends within society set the stage for small groups ►how you can use the four primary phases of group development to guarantee the right fit for every small-group member ►seven ways to cultivate a caring atmosphere ►five common problems to avoid ►the six foundational elements of every small group ►and much, much more!

Space is limited. Call (800) GRPS-R-US today for more information about seminars in your area.

(800) 477-7787, ask for offer **#303**

PILGRIMAGE
NAVPRESS
www.navpress.org